Psycho-nationalism

States routinely and readily exploit the grey area between sentiments of national affinity and hegemonic emotions geared to nationalist aggression. In this book, Arshin Adib-Moghaddam focuses on the use of Iranian identity to offer a timely exploration into the psychological and political roots of national identity and how these are often utilised by governments from East to West. Examining this trend, both under the Shah as well as by the governments since the 1979 Iranian revolution, Adib-Moghaddam's analysis is driven by what he terms 'psycho-nationalism', a new concept derived from psychological dynamics in the making of nations. Through this, he demonstrates how nationalist ideas evolved in global history and their impact on questions of identity, statecraft and culture. *Psycho-nationalism* describes how a nation is made, sustained and 'sold' to its citizenry and will interest students and scholars of Iranian culture and politics, world political history, nationalism studies and political philosophy.

ARSHIN ADIB-MOGHADDAM is Professor in Global Thought and Comparative Philosophies in the Department of Politics and International Studies at SOAS, University of London, and Chair of the Centre for Iranian Studies at the London Middle East Institute. In addition he was nominated Senior Associate Fellow at the Instituto Universitário de Lisboa (ISCTE-IUL), Center for International Studies, Portugal. He is the author of a number of books, including *On the Arab Revolts and the Iranian Revolution: Power and Resistance Today* (2013), and is the editor of *A Critical Introduction to Khomeini* (Cambridge University Press, 2014).

THE GLOBAL MIDDLE EAST

General Editors
Arshin Adib-Moghaddam, *SOAS, University of London*
Ali Mirsepassi, *New York University*

Editorial Advisory Board
Faisal Devji, *University of Oxford*
John Hobson, *University of Sheffield*
Firoozeh Kashani-Sabet, *University of Pennsylvania*
Zachary Lockman, *New York University*
Madawi Al-Rasheed, *King's College, University of London*
David Ryan, *University College Cork*

The Global Middle East series is a new book series that seeks to broaden and deconstruct the geographical boundaries of the 'Middle East' as a concept to include North Africa, Central and South Asia, as well as diaspora communities in Western Europe and North America. The series will feature fresh scholarship that employs theoretically rigorous and innovative methodological frameworks resonating across relevant disciplines in the humanities and the social sciences. In particular, the general editors welcome approaches that focus on mobility, the erosion of nation-state structures, travelling ideas and theories, transcendental techno-politics, the decentralisation of grand narratives and the dislocation of ideologies inspired by popular movements. The series will also consider translations of works by authors in these regions whose ideas are salient to global scholarly trends but are yet to be introduced to the Anglophone academy.

Psycho-nationalism
Global Thought, Iranian Imaginations

ARSHIN ADIB-MOGHADDAM
School of Oriental and African Studies, University of London

CAMBRIDGE
UNIVERSITY PRESS

University Printing House, Cambridge CB2 8BS, United Kingdom

One Liberty Plaza, 20th Floor, New York, NY 10006, USA

477 Williamstown Road, Port Melbourne, VIC 3207, Australia

314–321, 3rd Floor, Plot 3, Splendor Forum, Jasola District Centre, New Delhi – 110025, India

79 Anson Road, #06-04/06, Singapore 079906

Cambridge University Press is part of the University of Cambridge.

It furthers the University's mission by disseminating knowledge in the pursuit of education, learning, and research at the highest international levels of excellence.

www.cambridge.org
Information on this title: www.cambridge.org/9781108423076
DOI: 10.1017/9781108394918

© Arshin Adib-Moghaddam 2018

This publication is in copyright. Subject to statutory exception and to the provisions of relevant collective licensing agreements, no reproduction of any part may take place without the written permission of Cambridge University Press.

First published 2018

Printed in the United Kingdom by Clays, St Ives plc

A catalogue record for this publication is available from the British Library.

ISBN 978-1-108-42307-6 Hardback
ISBN 978-1-108-43570-3 Paperback

Cambridge University Press has no responsibility for the persistence or accuracy of URLs for external or third-party internet websites referred to in this publication and does not guarantee that any content on such websites is, or will remain, accurate or appropriate.

To Ghoncheh – beyond words.

Contents

	Introduction: Love and Politics	*page* 1
1	National Hysteria: Roma O' Morte	20
2	International Hubris: Kings of Kings and Vicegerents of God	45
3	Geographic Dislocations: Iran Is in India	68
4	Religious Neuroses: Islam and the People	89
5	Un-national Therapy: Freedom and Its Discontents	125
6	Sexing the Nation: Subversive Trans-localities	145
	Bibliography	159
	Index	167

Introduction: Love and Politics

The nation is a love story. At least this is how governments would like to have it because love for the nation is necessary to rule. To that end, governments have several 'romantic' devices to persuade. All governments use a range of national narratives imbued with emotional vigour and tantalising myths. At the time of writing, right-wing politicians are winning elections with the help of highly populist, almost hysterical themes such as 'making America great again', the winning campaign slogan of Donald Trump in the United States. These are the siren songs of (psycho-)nationalism. They are engineered to be persuasive enough to assail and conquer the cognition of the populace. Whether in Asia, Africa, America or Europe, one is continuously enticed to believe in the beauty of the nation. For example, in Britain the word 'Britannia' started as the Roman designation of the British Isles before it metamorphosed into a heroine of the seas in Elizabethan England and the emblem of the naval prowess of the British Empire two centuries later. Today, the idea and symbolism of Britannia has lost some of its meaning. Embattled as a national icon, much in the same way as the idea of Britain itself, the ideational stamina of Britannia has been affected by the historic vote to exit the European Union in June 2016 in the name of national sovereignty, which has led Welsh and Scottish nationalists to question the idea of the United Kingdom once again because they adhere to their own romanticised national myths. The point is that in the familial language of (psycho-)nationalism, in the United States, Britain and elsewhere, the nation is routinely represented almost like an irresistible muse, a siren song with distinctly emotional undertones. 'God bless America' – the target of such phrases is our state of mind and emotional habitat. My term 'psycho-nationalism' derives from such psychological dynamics. Government, the media, social networking sites, even popular culture in the form of soap operas and music have emerged as the primary carriers of the symbols of this emotive discourse. The target of these subtle forms of political manipulation is our mind and our emotions.

At the same time, the state hovers over a complex system in which psycho-nationalist narratives are moulded and implemented. Hence it claims the *Gewaltmonopol*, defined by German sociologist Max Weber as the monopoly of the legitimate use of physical force within a given territory. So if 'romantic' persuasion is not enough, if the siren song of the nation fails to entice, the nation-state can be enforced through violence, brute if necessary. You can be 'beaten' into submission. There are important differences in the ways in which state violence is implemented against assertive dissenters, but governments routinely crush opposition in the name of the nation. This systematic power is exercised through the machinery of laws, norms and regulations. If these strategies are not enough to deter a revolt, the state uses violence through its security forces, police, the military, etc. The Italian philosopher Giorgio Agamben remains firmly within the Eurocentric universe, but his focus on the 'state of exception' is a good conceptual tool for understanding this violence of state sovereignty.[1] The state allows itself to suppress. Thus, our lives are determined by this nation-state, whether we like it or not. From provisions for housing, university fees and food to war and peace, the nation-state continues to be a major factor in the lives of its citizens all over the world. In many ways the nation-state is more consequential in our lives than our parents. It 'stalks' us all the way to our living rooms, regulating everything from TV programmes to schooling issues. If this regulatory power, which always also includes surveillance, is not checked properly by civil society it threatens to turn into a form of arbitrary tyranny.

---

[1] See further Giorgio Agamben, *State of Exception*, Chicago: University of Chicago Press, 2005.

Therefore, this book takes seriously the power of the nation-state and modes of resistance to it. I will attempt to dislocate some of the debates on nationalism by investigating several 'sites' where 'psycho-nationalist' dynamics appear. I will keep a close eye on 'new', avant-garde disciplines such as global thought, global history and comparative philosophies, and my evidence is primarily discussed with reference to Iran. Admittedly, Iran is a convenient case study. In his influential book about nationalism, the late Eric Hobsbawm, Professor at Birkbeck and long-standing member of the British communist party, identified Iran as a 'relatively permanent political' unit alongside China, Korea, Vietnam and Egypt.[2] According to him, these countries 'had they been in Europe, would have been recognized as "historic nations"'. Hobsbawm mentioned Iran within the context of European imperialisms and movements that espoused nationalism as an anti-colonial strategy. According to him, the Iranian nation-state, as opposed to other 'entities' in the region that were a direct product of the Sykes-Pikot agreement, did not emerge out of imperial conquest. Rather, the idea of Iran pre-existed the short colonial interlude that created much of the so-called 'Middle East'.[3]

Certainly, Iran serves as a good example for the way the idea of a nation-state is created and sustained. But Hobsbawm and other European scholars of nationalism refer to the country only in passing, without much emphasis on the way Iran has been thought of and manufactured as a nation-state. In the absence of a critical review of the way Iran has been imagined, the country is wrongly assumed to be quintessentially Islamic, Shia, Persian or other. Therefore, what is needed, is an appreciation of the country that escapes the platitudes of 'identity'. If Iran has been invented as a 'historic nation' as Hobsbawm argues, then this history speaks to nationalism studies throughout the world. Yet the lack of emphasis on the country is also apparent

---

[2] Eric Hobsbawm, *Nations and Nationalism since 1780*, Cambridge: Cambridge University Press, 2nd edition, 2012, p. 137.
[3] See further Pinar Bilgin, 'Whose "Middle East"? Geopolitical Inventions and Practices of Security', *International Relations*, Vol. 18, No. 1, 2004, pp. 25–41.

in Hobsbawm's second pre-eminent publication in the field, *The Invention of Tradition*, which he edited with Terence Ranger, a passionate anti-colonial activist and Afrikanist who was deported from Southern Rhodesia (now Zimbabwe) by the white-minority government in 1963 because of his support of the African nationalist movement. Their study, with its emphasis on the role of the 'formalisation' and 'ritualisation' of traditions in the making of national myths, is required reading in most courses covering nationalisms today.[4] So if Iran is a relatively permanent political entity as Hobsbawm suggests, studying the traditions, norms and institutions of the country is a 'hard case' with which to gauge some of the mechanisms at work in the making of contemporary nation-states, even as they emerged in Europe and North America. In turn, this is important to assess how states control and manipulate their citizens. Hence, to understand psycho-nationalism, is to understand our daily lives and how the state impinges on everything that we do.

While I am certainly not claiming to present a comprehensive historical analysis (which has been provided by others), it is the task of this book to understand conceptually how the idea of Iran is created, in order to understand the mechanisms and effects of psycho-nationalist discourse.[5] At the same time, I am also paying attention to forms of resistance to those inventions which are engineered primarily by the state and its underbelly. The locus of psycho-nationalism, I claim, is the state; the language of resistance to it is spoken by actors within society. In this way, for instance, I discuss Ayatollah Khomeini, the late leader of the Iranian revolution, alongside Dariush Eghbali, the iconic Iranian pop singer who resides in exile in Los Angeles.

---

[4] Eric Hobsbawm and Terence Ranger (eds.), *The Invention of Tradition*, Cambridge: Cambridge University Press, 2012, p. 4.
[5] For rather more historical approaches see among others Ali Ansari, *The Politics of Nationalism in Modern Iran*, Cambridge: Cambridge University Press, 2012, and Firoozeh Kashani-Sabet, *Frontier Fictions: Shaping the Iranian Nation 1804–1946*, Princeton: Princeton University Press, 1999.

A second, rather more recent impetus for the idea that nations are invented came from Benedict Anderson. Comparable to Hobsbawm, Anderson only mentions Iran in passing when he discusses the impact of print-capitalism on the making of 'national' languages. He mentions how 'conscious' manipulations by the nationalists in the nineteenth and early twentieth century disturbed the relative unity of the 'Turkic speaking peoples' in Iran (Turkey, Iraq and the USSR). Turkish was appropriated as a European language through compulsory romanisation by Mustapha Kemal (Ataturk) in order to signify a 'Turkish' national consciousness 'at the expense of any wider Islamic identification'.[6] Language as a marker of a cloistered identity functioned in the same way in the USSR. The Russian communists first enforced 'an anti-Islamic, anti-Persian compulsory Romanisation' which was followed under Stalin in the 1930s by a 'Russifying compulsory Cyrillisation'.[7] Indeed, Russia looms large in the imagination of Iranian nationalists because of the treaties of Golestan (1813) and Turkmenchai (1828), according to which Iran lost all of its Caucasian territories, including contemporary Dagestan, eastern Georgia, Azerbaijan and Armenia, to the Russian empire. As one prominent professor at the University of Tehran put it: 'These humiliating events deeply shocked Iranian society and its political elite'.[8] Moreover, the Soviet Union plotted the occupation of northern Iran in 1946, one of the first crises diffused by the United Nation Security Council. Ultimately, Russian, British and US imperialism in the nineteenth and twentieth century facilitated the articulation of a 'postcolonial nationalism' in Iranian society that was opposed to foreign domination of the country. As we will see, after the revolution of 1979, the Iranian state readily stoked up and played to such sentiments.

---

[6] Benedict Anderson, *Imagined Communities: Reflections on the Origin and Spread of Nationalism*, London: Verso, 2016, pp. 45–6.
[7] Ibid., p. 46.
[8] Hamid Ahmadi, 'Islam and Nationalism in Contemporary Iranian Society and Politics', *Iranian Review of Foreign Affairs*, Vol. 1, No. 1, 2010, p. 201.

I have started with Hobsbawm and Anderson in order to ease the reader into the topic. There are at least four themes in the available literature on nationalism which their work touches upon, including studies about Iran. First, nationalism is largely treated as an elite project driven by the state and its underbelly. This emphasis on 'nationalism from above' is apparent in recent research by historians of contemporary Iran, whose contribution to the field traces ideational and institutional conceptions of the country.[9] Others have given particular attention to the blind spots of Iran's contemporary nationalist projects.[10] This scholarship covers a lot of ground in terms of both the role of the state in nationalist discourse and the impact of western modernity on the state-building process in Iran. And yet, the battlefield of nationalism is by far wider. Horizontally, the idea of Iran is a global phenomenon and has to be engaged with as such. Vertically, the idea of Iran has been inscribed into the very consciousness and body of Iranians. The psycho-nationalism of successive states ruling the Iranian terrain is cognitively intrusive and physically demanding. There is a physiognomy of Iran that has taken its psycho-somatic toll on the way Iran is imagined both within the country and elsewhere. As an invented mental space, psycho-nationalism in Iran represents a locus for identity, which is not merely cultural, civilisational or national. It is exactly personal because the 'modern' Iranian state has assaulted the cognition of its people on a deep psychological level. 'Cultural schizophrenia', in the words of the contemporary Iranian philosopher Daryush Shayegan, is a symptom of centuries-old psycho-nationalist dynamics which have affected the way Iranians perceive themselves and others.[11]

---

[9] See Ansari, *The Politics of Nationalism in Iran* and Kashani-Sabet, *Frontier Fictions*.

[10] See among others Rasmus Christian Elling, *Minorities in Iran: Nationalism and Ethnicity after Khomeini*, New York: Palgrave Macmillan, 2013; Alam Saleh, *Ethnic Identity and the State in Iran*, New York: Palgrave Macmillan, 2013 and Reza Zia-Ebrahimi, *The Emergence of Iranian Nationalism: Race and the Politics of Dislocation*, New York: Columbia University Press, 2016.

[11] See Dariush Shayegan, *Cultural Schizophrenia: Islamic Societies Confronting the West*, Syracuse: Syracuse University Press, 1997.

These coercive psycho-nationalist strategies by the state have been resisted in Iranian poetry, philosophy and popular culture. When the world-renowned diva of Iranian popular music Googoosh, who left Iran in 2000 after 20 years of artistic silence, called her comeback album 'Zoroaster', she was appropriating this ancient Iranian religion in protest against the Islamicised national narrative of the Islamic Republic. At least for Googoosh, the imagery of Zoroastrianism became a vehicle of protest much in the same way political interpretations of Islam became a carrier of resistance to the dictatorship of the Shah in the 1970s. This is not because she is a Zoroastrian 'fundamentalist'. Neither were the revolutionaries in 1979 particularly and coherently 'Islamic'. Such imageries and symbols of the past are used to call for an idea of Iran that safeguards diversity and multiculturalism. Before the revolution and after, there have been several revolts in the name of an inclusive and culturally tolerant idea of Iran and this power-resistance dialectic between the state and society has left an indelible imprint on the way Iran is perceived. In this way, Iran has become one of the most contested topics of contemporary global history. This is one of the reasons why Iranians that I have interviewed for this study – even second and third generation citizens in Europe and North America – find the country 'inescapable', 'mesmerising' and central to their personal identity.[12]

The primary material that I have gathered for this book through years of fieldwork in Iran and outside of the country shows the inherently global imagination that many Iranians hold. Many Iranians imagine the country in cosmopolitan and multicultural terms: Iran as the quintessential melting pot of world history, if you like.[13] Many others think the country as monolithic, either primarily 'Persian', 'Islamic' or 'Shia', or even French as the Shah once wrote

---

[12] Interviews with participants living in: Hamburg, 13 April 2016, Washington, DC, 26 June 2016, London, 16 August 2016. All respondents preferred to be anonymous.
[13] Ibid.

in *Life Magazine*.[14] This is why I approach the topic as an exercise in global thought and comparative philosophies. Iran as a subject matter stands at the crossroads of disciplines and theories. A pluralistic approach to the country ensures a pluralistic appreciation of its meanings. I have invented the 'fields of study' of 'Global Thought' and 'Comparative Philosophies' as a part of my academic title at the School of Oriental and African Studies (SOAS) in London. Much like an engineer of a mini state with one inhabitant (myself), I am now giving meaning to an invented outfit. Titles and corresponding 'identities' start with imagined ideas, even if they are entirely new as is my title. Nation-states follow a similar pattern. They are imagined and continuously filled with meaning. Therefore, I am presenting this study as a 'psycho-ethnography' of the way nation-states are imagined. Hence, this is not a project limited to Iran. It is research that contributes to a global understanding of nation-states and the psycho-nationalist politics that they pursue.

PSYCHO-NATIONALISM EXPLAINED

Even the most ardent 'globalist' who believes in the de-territorialisation of space, must be surprised that the nation continues to be presented, partially successfully, as a source of identity. When I was a student at the universities of Hamburg, America (Washington, DC) and Cambridge everyone spoke of the 'global village'. Conversely, studies into nationalism were outdated and largely confined to the postcolonial 'Third World'. There are nuances of course: national sentiments in North Korea are very different from those in Germany. The Supreme Leader of North Korea, Kim Jong-un propagates an aggressive nationalism. The German Chancellor Angela Merkel refrains from speaking about a 'German nation'. But it is rather surprising that even very intelligent people continue to defend national pride beyond innocent expressions of national affinity. This is largely

---

[14] Mohammad Reza Shah Pahlavi, 'A Future to Outshine Ancient Glories', *Life*, 31 May 1963.

because until very recently, nations were thought to be primordial and self-evident. In Europe and elsewhere, the nation was produced as a people with a common 'race', history, culture, set of habits and in particular with a shared language. In the course of the last four centuries, and in Europe certainly since the Treaty of Westphalia in 1648, the allegiance that used to tie communities to smaller polities such as city-states even within larger imperial entities, gradually came to be integrated into a tightly defined and formally delineated territory. In Iran this process was equally complicated. The position of the country at the crossroads of ancient human history forced successive leaders of the Iranian terrain to integrate and centralise a notion of Iran that would legitimise the ruler – a rather arduous task trying to unify the *satraps* and *ostans* that were ruled by the Cyruses, Xerxes, Dariuses, Alexanders and Gengis Khans of this world. And what to do with the loose ethno-geography of a place like that? The problem is exactly that the idea of Iran and its political management has an ancient genealogy. The point that I am making is that high politics in the region, including the politics of the nation, precede European modernity. It is just that the western archives haven't adequately captured this Iranian presence in global history.[15]

It is not then that the nation-state that came into existence through this process is a distinctly 'modern' phenomenon as Anderson, Gellner, Hobsbawm and Kedourie famously argue.[16] There were 'nationalised' entities in antiquity. Certainly, Sassanid Iran (224–651) had its own sense of the nation, with its own religious narrative (Zoroastrianism), symbolic capitol (Ctesiphon), official language (middle Persian) and Persian-centric ethno-ideology. But the absence of modern forms of communication such as the printing press, as Anderson argues, the 'techno-politics' of mass communication

---

[15] See further Arshin Adib-Moghaddam, 'A (Short) History of the Clash of Civilisations', *Cambridge Review of International Affairs*, Vol. 21, No. 2, 2006, pp. 217–34.
[16] Their writings are part and parcel of the many compilations in nationalism studies. See among others John Hutchinson and Anthony D. Smith (eds.), *Nationalism*, Oxford: Oxford University Press, 1994.

today and in particular recourse to ideological systems of psycho-controlling and monopolising the national narrative for the state made it that much more difficult to keep the nation together without the exercise of brute force and military dominance. In other words: modernity equipped the state with rather more sophisticated psycho-nationalist devices. In terms of dissemination and impact, mass producing pamphlets about the 'divine' rulership of the current Iranian leader Ali Khamenei in the seminaries of Qom, as well as his Twitter account with over 235,000 followers, is very different to propagating a divinely ordained universal order dominated by the king of kings, as Cyrus II proclaimed in the so-called 'Cyrus cylinder' in the sixth century BC. The psycho-nationalist *intention* is comparable, both strategies are meant to solicit submission to the ruler, but the ability of the ruling elites to get their message across is, of course, fundamentally different:[17] the Cyrus cylinder has been parked in the British Museum across from my office at SOAS on Russell Square, the Twitter account of Khamenei transcends spatial restriction.

We can agree that contemporary psycho-nationalism is distinctly invasive. Michel Foucault has termed such mature forms of political mind control 'bio-political'.[18] According to Foucault, bio-power is intimate; it targets our bodies. Despite his fascination for Iran during the revolutionary years of 1978–9, Foucault's empirical material remained Eurocentric. If he had studied the Iranian case beyond his journalistic articles for *Corriere della Serra* in Italy, Foucault would have discovered how state power in Iran failed to 'discipline' and subdue resistance.[19] Bio-power in Iran, which has been implemented through ideological education and measures to optimise the penetrability of the population through psychological

---

[17] See further Arshin Adib-Moghaddam, 'What Is Radicalism? Power and Resistance in Iran', *Middle East Critique*, Vol. 21, No. 3, 2012, pp. 271–90.

[18] See among other works Michel Foucault, *The Birth of Biopolitics: Lectures at the College de France, 1978–1979*, New York: Palgrave Macmillan, 2010.

[19] See further Arshin Adib-Moghaddam, *On the Arab Revolts and the Iranian Revolution: Power and Resistance Today*, New York: Bloomsbury, 2013, Chapter 4.

control, has not brought about political uniformity and subjectification. The emphasis of Foucault on Europe brought with it overindulgence in the power of capitalism and its disciplinary effects on the individual. According to Foucault, modern forms of (neo)liberal capitalism determine us all the way down to our bodies, even our sexual preferences. In countries such as Iran, however, (neo)liberal capitalism has never really determined subjectivity. Even the introduction of neo-liberal economic policies in the 1990s and the shift away from a Islamo-socialist, state-centred economy to an increasingly capitalist system has not 'normalised' state–society relations. So where there is bio-power, there is also resistance, and where there is psycho-nationalism, there is opposition.[20]

In Iran, psycho-nationalism has been pursued not only as a very sophisticated strategy of control over bodies and individual conduct. Psycho-nationalism is a cognitive strategy. From the Achaemenidian idea of metaphysical kingship which was plagiarised in the twentieth century by the Pahlavi dynasty to the Islamicised, Platonic philosopher-king which entered the doctrine of Ayatollah Khomeini in the form of the rule of the 'Supreme Leader' underpinning the constitution of the Islamic Republic today, the efforts to discipline the people living under the jurisdiction of successive Iranian states have been intrusive. In this process, cognition is targeted; it is given a hegemonic role. Psycho-nationalism attempts to rule over the meaning of the national narrative and it is within this dense psychological space that the strategic surveillance as well as the counter-tactics of resistance reveal themselves. Today, psycho-nationalism attempts to extend the sovereignty of the state and turns citizens into objects of power. Ideally, psycho-nationalism surrenders citizens out of free will. Once we are psychologically coded, we lay down our arms voluntarily.

---

[20] For recent engagements with Foucault with a particular emphasis on his writings about Iran see Behrooz Ghamari-Tabrizi, *Foucault in Iran: Islamic Revolution after the Enlightenment*, Minneapolis: University of Minnesota Press, 2016 and Jason Bahbak Mohaghegh, *Silence in Middle Eastern and Western Thought: The Radical Unspoken*, London: Routledge, 2013.

But this effort to turn us into compliant subjects is routinely resisted by those pockets of society that try to escape such psycho-nationalist dynamics. Once this dialectic is understood, it becomes clearer why recent resistance to the state in Britain emerged from the ghettoised youth in North London on the one side, and university students on the other. Both 'spaces' of society are relatively unfazed about the machinations of state power. The former because the state and its police force are deemed discriminatory and racist, the latter because of similar reasons and a quasi-liberal sense of entitlement. In Iran in 1979, the revolution was driven by similar strata of society. It was primarily the university students and the workers who created the largest demonstrations in human history. Given that their movement was transversal, that is, it cut through all layers of Iranian society, the revolution gained momentum. This is one of the major differences between a local riot and a transnational revolution.[21]

In its very essence the nation is an empty space and there has been continuous resistance to state-engineered (psycho)nationalisms from 'below'. There is no reality to any nation beyond inventions of the human mind. In essence, the nation-state is like my academic title. It was created at some stage and then it developed a life of its own. This understanding of nations as imaginary constructs developed more forcefully towards the end of the twentieth century. Several western scholars (e.g. Anderson, Gellner, Hobsbawm) supported the notion that nations are concocted, either through textual representations, inventions of identity or more generally through culture. In Europe, before this hiatus, nations were taken as a given. They were assumed to be primordial; a fact of human existence that was necessary. Even though it has become a cliché, John Lennon was correct to assume that imagining and then living a borderless life would minimise the power of the state. Without strong sentiments towards the nation, the sovereignty of states loosens. Where there is

---

[21] I have conceptualised the term further in *On the Arab Revolts and the Iranian Revolution*, 2013.

a nation, there must be a state. Where there is a state, there must be a nation to be ruled. Understanding this dialectic contributes to understanding one of the main factors of human existence today.

Drawing from the Iranian experience, this book dissects some of the sites where this 'nation-state' is produced. On a more general, conceptual level, it identifies what I call psycho-nationalist dynamics in the production of nation-states. By psycho-nationalism, I am not referring to an innocent sense of belonging, the affinity with national folklore, or the nation as an administrative and institutional point of reference. You are not a psycho-nationalist if you are Iranian and love the poetry of Hafiz, the aesthetics of Isfahan, the popular songs of the LA-based singer Dariush or the architectural splendour of Persepolis. However, the borderlines between 'national pride' and what I call psycho-nationalism are thin. States routinely and readily exploit the grey zone that opens up between innocent sentiments of national affinity and hegemonic emotions geared to nationalist aggression. Love for the nation, after all, almost always ends tragically; the kind of psycho-nationalism that I am talking about in this book is a destructive sentiment.

Yet, psycho-nationalism remains one of the most potent forces in human history, certainly in the modern period and in our current seemingly 'post-modern' condition. At the time of writing, right-wing politicians in Europe and the United States are stoking up fears and xenophobia as a winning formula at the ballot box. US President Donald Trump, for instance, has called for a ban on Muslims entering the United States and a wall to keep Mexican immigrants out of the country. His campaign slogan, 'making America great again', is a typical connection between the nation and sentiments expressing superiority to other peoples. In Europe, right-wing leaders such as Marine Le Pen in France are winning elections on the back of anti-immigrant and distinctly psycho-nationalistic slogans and imagery. The flag and the hymn, it seems, are celebrating a surprising comeback. Of course, if you love Paris as the quintessential manifestation of French *savoir vivre* you are not a psycho-nationalist. But if this sentiment turns into rejection of those who you do not consider to be French, then you are cultivating a destructive attitude. Psycho-nationalism does to thinking what orthodox historians and philosophers do to the history of other peoples: it keeps them out.

Psycho-nationalism is a source of identity for all of those who are considered a part of the in-group or 'imagined community', while it fosters intolerance and hate towards those who do not belong to it. People who think beyond identities and strict group affiliations are psychologically relieved of such destructive feelings, which the founder of Psychoanalysis Sigmund Freud (1856–1939) would have called 'libidinous' in Vienna back in the early twentieth century. Throughout this book, I will equip myself with poetry, selected philosophical traditions and other forms of life-affirming thoughts and practice to dismiss the notion that we have to feel the nation, and that we have to love it beyond our own lives and existence.

Psycho-nationalism is about 'othering'. It is about delineating the community (or in-group) from the ones who are not thought to be part of it due to racial, linguistic, ethnic or other reasons. Freud explains hostility against people of other races, religion and nations in terms of narcissism: 'In the undisguised antipathies and aversions which people feel towards strangers with whom they have to do, we may recognize the expression of self-love – of narcissism'.[22] Psycho-nationalism has certainly a lot to do with an irrational love for the nation, which implies love for the 'self'. The narcissistic gain catered for by psycho-nationalist propaganda is clear. It suggests that you are better. The followers of the community (or in-group), simply by belonging to it, are thought to be purer, greater and superior to those who are outside of the group who become the objects of psycho-nationalist mind control. This is called 'positive distinction' in social psychology. Indeed, neuro-physiological research claims a strong connection between the brain and this urge to make ourselves feel better

---

[22] Sigmund Freud, *The Complete Psychological Works of Sigmund Freud*, Vol. 18, London: Vintage, 2001, p. 102.

in comparison to others. So if you think yourself superior to other people in West Asia and North Africa simply because you think you are 'purely Iranian', then you are trying to elevate yourself to a higher status; you are distinguishing your 'self' in opposition to the 'inferior' other. This could also be caused by self-hate and not narcissism as Freud assumes. For if you are comfortable with your identity, why would you want to proclaim your superiority in the first place?

One of the central arguments that I intend to pursue in this book is immediately related to what I have just extracted with reference to my understanding of psycho-nationalism. The Iranian case shows in a very illuminating way how states pursue the politics of identity in order to sustain their legitimacy to rule. In that regard, Iran is a typical nation-state and Eric Hobsbawm is probably right to identify the country as a 'relatively permanent' historic nation, as indicated.[23] Certainly, the Iranian national narrative has been evident since antiquity. Iran has been imagined almost throughout global history. With this historical legacy (some would call it a burden) comes an intense focus on what it means to be Iranian. The lines of division between those who claim to speak for Iran and those who live in Iran as citizens on a daily basis have been strictly drawn by successive states ruling the country. Self and other are not distinguished merely in terms of Iran and the rest of the world. The main problem in contemporary Iranian history is the political divisions that hegemonic, state-centred national narratives created *within* the country. Today, the elites governing the Islamic Republic differentiate between *khodi* (those who belong to the revolutionary core) and the *gheire khodi*, essentially the rest of humanity including Iranian reformists, the 'west', etc., who become the targets of propaganda and ideological manipulation. Psycho-nationalist methods and procedures are at the heart of keeping this distinction functional for the state. This book is about revealing some of them.

[23] Hobsbawm, *Nations and Nationalism*, p. 137.

Psycho-nationalism is a division-creating device. The Islamic revolution of 1979, like any other massive upheaval in global history, was all about creating ideational difference. The narcissistic gain suggested by the revolutionary leaders, that Iran is the vanguard of a global revolution of the oppressed, was meant to suggest to their followers that simply by belonging to the revolution they would be more pious, purer and morally superior to the rest of the world who were by definition excluded from this process of self-fulfilment. This is why for the deep state in Iran, certainly for the core of the Revolutionary Guards and the Baseej who support the theocratic establishment led by the Supreme Leader Ayatollah Ali Khamenei, criticism of the state is synonymous with betrayal of the nation. Research into totalitarianism in Germany offers some clues as to why there is such rage against people with a different view and lifestyle. In the words of Theodor Adorno, one of the chief critical theorists of the Frankfurt School: criticising the 'in-group' 'is resented as a narcissistic loss and elicits rage'.[24] A totalitarian structure based on supreme truths cannot afford 'what they deem *zersetzend*, that which debunks their own stubbornly maintained values and it also explains the hostility of prejudiced persons against any kind of introspection'.[25] The Persian word for *zersetzend* is *fetnehgar* or seditionists, which is the exact reference given to the leaders of the so-called Green Movement and others who were a part of the massive demonstrations against the government of the former Iranian President Mahmoud Ahmadinejad in 2009. As Ahmadinejad pronounced at the time: 'The nation's huge river would not leave any room for the expression of dirt and dust' accusing his opponents of 'officially recognising thieves, homosexuals and scumbags'.[26] Psycho-nationalists are averse to complexity,

---

[24] Theodor W. Adorno, *The Culture Industry: Selected Essays on Mass Culture*, London: Routledge, 1991, p. 145.
[25] Ibid.
[26] 'The Dust Revolution – How Mahmoud Ahmadinejad's Jibe Backfired', *The Guardian*, 18 June 2009. Available at www.theguardian.com/world/2009/jun/18/iran-election-protests-mahmoud-ahmadinejad (accessed 21 January 2016).

dissent, diversification and a multicultural, multi-sexual composition of society. Ultimately, they adhere to a rather patronising notion of politics that is based on sophisticated forms of divide and rule tactics.

I began this book with a short sketch of global flashpoints of psycho-nationalism and brought the discussion closer to the Iranian case. In the midst of the current cultural reconfigurations, partially provoked by immigration patterns that defy borders, notions of nationhood – including as we have seen psycho-nationalist ones proclaimed by the right-wing – are celebrating a comeback. In largely secular societies in Europe and North America, psycho-nationalism continues to fill the void left behind by other forms of identification, including organised religion. In most societies with an instilled sense of nationhood, including in seemingly religious ones such as Iran, the idea of a national community addresses the need to belong and turns such sentiments into powerful drivers of 'national and personal identity'. This powerful re-emergence of the idea of the nation in response to processes of de-territorialisation and transnational dynamics has been compared to the period of the emergence of the contemporary nation-state from the mid-nineteenth century that I explored above. Then and now, psycho-nationalism fulfils a sense-giving mission. Homi Bhaba correctly observes in this regard that in situations like this, the 'nation fills the void left in the uprooting of communities and kin, and turns that loss into the language of metaphor'.[27]

Yet, perhaps this discourse is not so much metaphorical but psychological. Metaphors certainly propel the nation along a wide space, along 'distances and cultural differences that span the imagined community of the nation-people'.[28] But in order to function adequately, the idea of the nation needs a powerful cognitive momentum, a 'psycho-discourse' penetrative enough to assault the senses of its citizens. Psycho-nationalism, indeed, is about life and

---

[27] Homi K. Bhabha, *The Location of Culture*, London: Routledge, 1994, p. 200.
[28] Ibid.

death. Soldiers die for the 'motherland'. The main ministries and government institutions all over the world tend to be surrounded by statues and monuments commemorating 'the fallen', certainly at Whitehall in London, in Washington DC, Moscow and Tehran. Accordingly, national *sentiments*, itself a term that alludes to psychological dynamics, have to be coded in order to accept this sacrifice. This dynamic may have been *perfected* very recently in human history, but the idea that it came about merely in the wake of European 'modernity' in the nineteenth century is false and an unfortunate residue of Eurocentric scholarship.

Which parameters qualify my term psycho-nationalism further? I am certainly not implying that Iran or any other country is 'abnormal'. Psycho-nationalism refers to a discourse and truth regime driven by powerful actors, in particular the state and its underbelly which is aimed at affecting and codifying the cognition of receptive objects within the nation and other potential targets beyond. I will unravel and explain the intricacies of this conceptualisation along empirical examples throughout this book. Suffice to add at this stage, that several studies about Iran have established that idioms and norms such as blood, martyrdom (the so-called Kerbala paradigm), sacrifice, God or religion more generally have been employed by the Islamic Republic to simulate the idea of a national community with transnational appeal.[29] In this usage of grand concepts, some with a clear imperial ambition as I will argue in Chapter 2, the post-revolutionary Iranian state does not differ fundamentally from the ancien régime of the Shah. Both the monarchic sovereignty principle in Iranian history and the theocratic one claim a distinctly imperial and hegemonic prerogative to rule. In this way Iran's psycho-nationalism is steeped in a sense of imperial grandeur that makes this case comparable to other revolutionary countries of modernity, certainly Russia and China.[30]

---

[29] See among others Nikki R. Keddie, *Religion and Politics in Iran: Shi'ism from Quietism to Revolution*, New Haven: Yale University Press, 1983.

[30] For a comparative study see Ghoncheh Tazmini, *Revolution and Reform in Russia and Iran: Modernisation and Politics in Revolutionary States*, London: I.B. Tauris, 2012.

And yet at the same time, an analysis of psycho-nationalism driven by the state and its shadows within society has to include the element of resistance. In many ways psycho-nationalism in Iran has merely created what may be called a 'quasi nation'. In this sense, psycho-nationalism can be singled out for what it does not do: integrate, ameliorate, harmonise, assimilate. The language of psycho-nationalism, we will see in Chapters 3 and 4, is littered with blind spots and marginalisations despite its overarching effort to discipline society and to create a functioning and ideal *homo Islamicus*. I will show in Chapter 5 how Iranian intellectuals and civil society activists questioned the tenets of that official discourse from the outset of the revolution. At the heart of the dialectics between state and society, it is argued in this chapter, lies the struggle for freedom in Iran, which is codified in a rather more cosmopolitan, tolerant, liberal, secular and inclusive national narrative. Therefore, we are dealing with very sophisticated inventions that are meant to create the mirage of nationhood. Primarily, this book is about unravelling some of them in the Iranian context. I intend to show how this nation has been enacted cognitively, to discover some under-researched sites and sounds that make the Iranian narrative rhyme. Stripped off its layers of constructed meanings, Iran is as soulless, deserted and vacant a space as any other nation. The real meaning of the country cannot be found in discourse, institutions or national anthems. It is the everyday life of Iranians that is real; it is the trials and tribulations of our daily affairs that give any nation its real meaning and purpose. Everything else is concocted for the nefarious purpose of political power.

1 National Hysteria: Roma O' Morte

Roma o' Morte, Rome or death, proclaimed General Giuseppe Garibaldi in typical 'psycho-nationalist' parlance in the late nineteenth century, at once linking the 'eternal city' to notions of blood and sacrifice in order to consolidate the *risorgimento* or unification of Italy in the face of foreign invasion and internal strife. Similarly dramatic emotions were expressed by his contemporaries, in particular Giuseppe Mazzini (1805–72), probably Italy's most famous nationalist. Sceptical of communist calls for a worker's revolution in Italy – Karl Marx referred to him as a middle-class reactionary – the discourse used by Mazzini is typically emotional, imbued with themes such as God, sacrifice, love, death, blood, kinship and unity.[1] 'Love your country', he demanded from his listeners during a speech in 1848 in protest of the killing of Italian soldiers by Austrian forces.[2] 'Your country is the land where your parents sleep, where is spoken that language in which the chosen of your heart blushing whispered the first word of love'. This romantic, almost poetic reference, which seems rather innocent at first sight, is immediately followed by a prescription to give blood for the nation: 'It is your name, your glory, your sign among the peoples. Give to it your thought, your counsel, your blood . . . Let it be one, as the thought of God'.[3]

Mazzini was certainly not a fascist, despite the appropriation of his thought by Benito Mussolini and some recent scholarship

---

[1] 'Interview with Karl Marx, head of L'internationale'. Available at www.hartford-hwp.com/archives/26/020.html (accessed 21 February 2016).

[2] Giuseppe Mazzini, 'To the Young Men of Italy', in Lewis Copeland, Lawrence W. Lamm and Stephen J. McKenna (eds.), *The World's Great Speeches*, Mineola: Dover Publications, 1999, p. 101.

[3] Ibid.

linking his ideas to the latter.⁴ His nationalism was tempered given that he embedded it in a humanitarian discourse. But his constant reference to Europe as the pinnacle of civilisation and his repeated emphasis on blood sacrifice as a necessary ingredient in the making of nations, lent itself to abuse in post-unification Italy, including by the fascist movement. The mobilisation of the masses to safeguard the honour of the nation, his intense emphasis on the role of God, transmuted into a secular form of theo-politics. As a consequence, the national narrative was given a sacrosanct status which was readily exploited by those who claimed to work in the name of the nation and as its chaperone. Mazzini believed that Italy could only be adequately united through heroism, sacrifice and martyrdom, symbols and imagery that were very central to his dramatic reading of national regeneration. Once this task was accomplished, Mazzini promised, Italy would lead Europe to civilisational greatness. These are typically psycho-nationalist themes and they fed into the mythology of the fascist movement after the First World War, when motives such as blood and sacrifice for the nation and unity in the name of a pure race became particularly dominant in the public psyche throughout Europe. As *Il fascio*, the Fascist's main organ in Italy proclaimed in 1921: 'The Holy Communion of war has moulded us all with the same mettle of generous sacrifice'.⁵

The German experience in the late nineteenth and early twentieth century is comparable. In Germany too, the themes appropriated by Mazzini – purity, blood, sacrifice, honour, unity – played a pivotal role in cementing the idea of a nation. Johann Gottlieb von Fichte (1762–1814) is probably the most famous forerunner to these themes that I have termed 'psycho-nationalist' because of their emotional charge and their cognitive power. Fichte started out as a supporter

---

⁴ See further Simon Levis Fullam, *Giuseppe Mazzini and the Origins of Fascism*, New York: Palgrave Macmillan, 2015 and Simonetta Falasca-zamponi, *Fascist Spectacle: The Aesthetics of Power in Mussolini's Italy*, London: University of California Press, 2000.
⁵ In Mark Antliff, *Avant-garde Fascism: The Mobilisation of Myth, Art and Culture in France, 1909–1939*, Durham: Duke University Press, 2007, p. 38.

of the French revolution, in particular its calls for cosmopolitanism. Like Mazzini, Fichte was not a bigoted nationalist, but his emphasis on the superiority of German culture and language was used by latter generations in order to put forward an ethnocentric idea of Germany. If Mazzini accentuated the glory of Rome, the city of love and empires, Fichte maintained that Germans should assert leadership of Europe (and by implication the world) because of the purity of the German language which he deemed free of Latin influence. According to him, this undiluted linguistic heritage allowed German philosophers to express their ideas without mediation and in a clear and rational format. Again, quite similar to Mazzini, Fichte attributed theological greatness to the German nation which he deemed blessed by a godly (göttlich) spirit and a distinct (Eigentümlich) national character. Because of their special status, Germans had emerged as the *Urvolk* or archetype nation of humankind. The psycho-nationalist terminology is apparent here: godly, pure, national character (*Volkstum*), spiritual (geistig), death, blood, sacrifice. Fichte turned being German from a simple geographic designation into a matter of life and death, into a primordial and unique 'identity' with frightening cognitive force. In his own words: '(und dass) ein wahrhafter Deutscher nur könne leben wollen, um eben Deutscher zu sein und zu bleiben und die Seinigen zu ebensolchen zu bilden'. [(and that) a true German could only want to live, in order to be- and remain German, and to educate his own to be the same].[6]

The prescription to delineate a German self, unpolluted from foreign (ausländisch) influence, despite the non-militaristic approach that Fichte borrowed from the progressive adherents to the Enlightenment, nonetheless set the precedent for the racialised language pursued by German thinkers such as Ernst Bergman (1881–1945) in the late nineteenth century and the beginning of the

---

[6] In Felicity Rash, *German Images of the Self and the Other: Nationalist, Colonialist and Anti-semitic Discourse 1871–1918*, New York: Palgrave Macmillan, 2012, p. 41 (my translation).

twentieth century.[7] This is the time period when psycho-nationalist concepts matured into pseudo-scientific theories that charged traditional forms of nationalism with immense cognitive force, powerful enough to galvanise fascist movements to power all over the world. In the German case, Fichte and to a lesser extent Herder and even Otto von Bismarck, the Prussian Duke who coined the famous militaristic credo *Blut und Boden* (blood and soil), were increasingly appropriated by Nazi sympathisers for ideological purposes. Indeed, the aforementioned Ernst Bergman used his professorship at the University of Leipzig to embrace Fichte as the main forerunner of National Socialism in Germany.[8] Comparable to Italy, war was a catalyst for radicalisation. Bergman wrote his first book about Fichte in the aftermath of the First World War and Germany's punishing defeat. Like Mazzini who was appropriated by the Italian fascists, Fichte became the poster-child for the Nazis because of his emphasis on blood, honour, national character, educational and physical perfection and national resurrection. Psycho-nationalism, then, carries a blood-stained genealogy that was readily exploited by the state. It was born in a period of immense global turmoil, war and revolutionary upheaval. Hence it is certainly not, even in its contemporary manifestations, a recipe for democracy, pluralism and social empowerment. Neither Mazzini, nor Fichte are good reference points for a functioning, inclusive and tolerant society.

There are several more examples that will pave the way for a better understanding of psycho-nationalism. There is this metaphysical assurance that it conveys a sense of romantic belonging and rooting of identity which is comforting to many individuals even if it is a false promise. Certainly, when the famed French philosopher Ernest Renan entered the lecture hall at the Sorbonne on 11 March 1882 to ruminate about the question *qu'est-ce qu'une nation* (what is a

---

[7] See further Yvonne Sherratt, *Hitler's Philosophers*, New Haven: Yale University Press, 2013.

[8] See Ernst Bergman, *Fichte und der Nationalsozialismus*, Breslau: Walter Gehl und Johann Koch, 1933, especially pp. 6–8.

nation), he must have felt that he was speaking as an unmistakeable 'Frenchman', that his whole existence was typically 'French'. Despite his scepticism towards definitions of nations that are framed with reference to 'race, language, material interest, religious affinities, geography, and military necessity',[9] Renan accentuated the contingency of France and other 'primary nations' such as Russia, Germany and England. 'A nation is a soul, a spiritual principle' he famously proclaimed. 'The nation, like the individual, is the culmination of a long past of endeavours, sacrifice, and devotion'. As such it is by far more abstract and in its metaphysical essence by far more valuable than its material base. 'A heroic past, great men, glory . . . this is the social capital upon which one bases a national idea'. According to Renan, a nation is the surface effect of a common past, a shared heritage that is signposted by common battles and glorious achievements. 'To have common glories in the past and to have a common will in the present; to have performed great deeds together, to wish to perform still more – these are the essential conditions for being a people'. And what are those great deeds, what is strong enough to bind this metaphysical collective together beyond time and space? According to Renan, a nation should be repeatedly marched through a valley of tears: 'suffering in common unifies more than joy does. Where national memories are concerned, griefs are of more value than triumphs, for they impose duties, and require a common effort'. While nations have an objective existence, they are not primordial. Moreover, while nations may merge in the future under French-European leadership, 'at the present time, the existence of nations is a good thing, a necessity even. Their existence is the guarantee of liberty, which would be lost if the world had only one law and only one master'.[10]

In similar fashion compared to Mazzini and Fichte, psychonationalism reveals itself in Renan's thought as typically emotional.

---

[9] Ernest Renan, 'What Is a Nation', text of a conference delivered at the Sorbonne on 11 March 1882. Available at http://ucparis.fr/files/9313/6549/9943/What_is_a_Nation.pdf (accessed 12 June 2016).
[10] Ibid.

It is interesting to note that all three authors put particular emphasis on martyrdom, a 'complex' that contemporary scholars repeatedly attribute to a particularly Islamic and Shia expression of politics.[11] But at this stage we can distil a few more pointers about the genealogy of psycho-nationalism, certainly in the way it appeared in Europe primarily in the nineteenth century. First, there is a very particular and recurrent link between the nation and individual emotions such as honour, pride and love. This reveals the Cartesian enlightenment tradition and its anthropocentric perspective at the heart of psycho-nationalist discourse. Hence, the nation is not only a metaphysical principle without linkage to the fate of the individual. Psycho-nationalism ties the individual, the 'man' – in truly phallocentric European tradition – to the very essence of the nation, its heritage, present and future. In the words of Renan: 'A large aggregate of men, healthy in mind and warm of heart, creates the kind of moral conscience which we call a nation'.[12] As such, the individual is reminded that he has a particular duty to safeguard the sovereignty of the nation, for its existence and viability is concomitant with his own.

Secondly, there is certainly the emotional aspect, which I have already reiterated several times. But beyond this constant emphasis on blood and identity, psycho-nationalism is dependent on a very modern belief in the possibility of change or a utopia which can be achieved in the here and now and which is not postponed to the 'other-worldly'. In this sense psycho-nationalism is particularly 'positivist'; it affords its carriers the possibility of achievement. People have to believe in the possibility of the task and psycho-nationalism became a perfect mirage to intoxicate the masses into believing in the promise of total change. To that end, people had to be coded to believe in a better tomorrow through formal re-education – Mazzini and Fichte were great advocates of a new 'national' school curriculum

---

[11] See further Edward Said, *Covering Islam: How the Media and the Experts Determine How We See the Rest of the World*, London: Vintage, 1997.
[12] Renan, 'What Is a Nation?'

and the physical re-education of the individual into 'healthy' and functioning citizens. All of these mechanisms were particularly psychological; they were meant to reform thinking and they continue to have an impact on the way politics is absorbed and processed cognitively today.

EASTERN PRECEDENTS

There is controversy over the genealogy of nationalist thinking in Iran (and the Arab world) in the scholarly literature. But in general, research in Europe and North America tends to locate the emergence of 'modern' nationalism in the so-called 'west'. In a rather more critical study of the subject matter, it is observed that the 'west' saw nationalism as the 'quintessential expression of inclusive tolerance. And this image was then often reinforced by a distinction between the West's "civic" nationalism and illiberal "ethnic" nationalism'.[13] The non-western world was juxtaposed to this self-image: 'As the central organising principle of modern politics, nationalism was thus dichotomized between a noble Western invention and an ignoble non-Western imitation'.[14]

While there is overlap due to the intense dialectic between 'East' and 'West' during the colonial period which created common Euro-Asian spaces, it is principally problematic to reduce the emergence of nationalism to European ideas. The concept of an organised community is central to the canons of eastern philosophy and its *belles-lettres*. As an example of the latter, the Muslim philosopher Ibn Khaldun (d.1406) redefined 'asabiyya' (social solidarity) from its pre-Islamic origin and Quranic legacy, in the first systematic sociological conceptualisation of a polity in his famous *Muqaddimah* (Introduction to history) as early as in 1377 AD. Ibn Khaldun followed the line of classical philosophers of the Muslim enlightenment, such as

---

[13] Anthony W. Marx, *Faith in Nation: Exclusionary Origins of Nationalism*, Oxford: Oxford University Press, 2005, p. vii.
[14] Ibid., p. viii.

Abu Nasr Farabi, Razi, Ibn Sina (Avicenna) and Ibn Rushd (Averroes). Like them, he was a distinctly original and cosmopolitan thinker who took full advantage of the pan-Islamic currents of the period. His inclusive conceptualisation of a social community comes out in his depiction of the non-Arab 'other', in this case the 'Persians':

> Thus the founders of grammar were Sibawaih and after him, al-Farisi and Az-Zajjaj. All of them were of non-Arab (Persian) descent . . . They invented rules of (Arabic) grammar . . . great jurists were Persians . . . only the Persians engaged in the task of preserving knowledge and writing systematic scholarly works. Thus the truth of the statement of the prophet becomes apparent, 'If learning were suspended in the highest parts of heaven the Persians would attain it' . . . The intellectual sciences were also the preserve of the Persians, left alone by the Arabs, who did not cultivate them . . . as was the case with all crafts . . . This situation continued in the cities as long as the Persians and Persian countries, Iraq, Khorasan and Transoxiana, retained their sedentary culture.[15]

According to Khaldun, asabiyya (social solidarity) is an important factor in the cyclical rise and fall of civilisations and empires. Good governance enhances the social solidarity of the community. Ideally, this socially constructed, politically administered consciousness would strengthen the community against external aggression and internal subversion. Here, Ibn Khaldun reveals himself as a theorist of state power. The more the state is able to foster this sense of tribal community and kinship, the more likely it is to survive the vicissitudes of history. In a clear re-conceptualisation of Aristotle's notion of *koinonia*, Khaldun emphasises the importance of social organisation (or *ijtima*) for this dialectical interaction between state and society. Human social organisation (*al-ijtima al-insani*)

---

[15] Ibn Khaldun, *The Muqaddimah: An Introduction to History, Vol. 1*, translated by Franz Rosenthal, Princeton: Princeton University Press, 1989, pp. 429–30.

would be moulded by this ideal state in order to bring out the inherently civilised (*madani*) nature of the citizenry. Khaldun wrote during a period of internal division of the Muslim empire partially caused by external threats. While he had a clear interest in re-inscribing the authority of the state as a prophylaxis to internal divisions, he emphasised that no state can exist without fostering social cohesion among its citizenry. Hence, Khaldun shared this preoccupation about the social construction and maintenance of a community with western theorists of modernity, such as Emile Durkheim and Ernest Gellner:

> Both Ibn Khaldun and Ernest Gellner have developed persuasive theoretical models that challenge such views and place group solidarity at the heart of long-term social change. Moreover, their work demonstrates how difficult it is to generate and maintain cohesive networks of individuals over longer periods of time, and how changed social conditions profoundly affect patterns of group solidarity: while for Ibn Khaldun the opulent urban lifestyles inevitably corrode social cohesion built in the shared ascetic living of tribal warriors, for Gellner modernity forges a new form of solidarity built around the promise of continuous economic growth, moral equality and cultural homogeneity among citizens inhabiting their own nation-state.[16]

Even Ibn-Khaldun's largely sober and research-led inquiries about world history were abused as tropes in psycho-nationalist narratives. As discussed above, Ibn Khaldun was a complex thinker, whose concepts were nuanced and balanced. He did not have a dichotomous notion of self and other, or an aggressive manifesto for political action. And yet, he became a major reference point in the discourse of Arab nationalists, in particular at the beginning of the twentieth century when Arab nationalism was sponsored by British and French

---

[16] Sinisa Malesevic, 'Where Does Group Solidarity Come From? Gellner and Ibn Khaldun Revisited', *Thesis Eleven: Critical Theory and Historical Sociology*, Vol. 129, No. 1, p. 97.

imperial strategists as a means to weaken the Ottoman Empire.[17] For instance, in the voluminous writings of Sati Al-Husri (1882–1962), the Ottoman-Syrian nationalists whose ideas became a pillar of Ba'thist ideology, Ibn Khaldun appears as a purveyor of Arab nationalism. Al-Husri borrowed generously from the German romanticists, von Ranke and Fichte, in his reinvention of Khaldun as an Arab nationalist. In typically psycho-nationalist fashion, he reconceptualised asabiyya as a spiritual bond among the members of a nation which is defined in terms of language and a shared memory or historical consciousness. According to this view, there is a metaphysical kinship between society and the nation.

In al-Husri (and his contemporaries such as Michel Aflaq), we find all the ingredients characteristic of psycho-nationalism that I have discussed so far: the nation is represented as the protective mother that Arabs need to honour and sacrifice for; love for the nation entices the individual to unite and fight for a better, utopian tomorrow; nationalism motivates 'just' struggles and revolts; politics is configured as an arena of blood, sacrifice and honour; passion is presented as a potent psycho-cognitive force with an ideological edge.[18] In the words of al-Husri: 'We must remember that the nationalist idea enjoys a *self-motivating power*; it is a *driving impulse* to action and to struggle. When it *enters the mind* and dominates the soul it is one of the *motive ideas* . . . which *awakens* the people and inspires them to sacrifice'.[19] The psychological elements are obvious here and they are far removed from anything Ibn Khaldun had to say about politics in general and asabiyya in particular. Al-Husri is clearly constructing a psychologised narrative, dotted with anthropomorphic

---

[17] See further Nurullah Ardlc, 'Genealogy or *Asabiyya?* Ibn Khaldun between Arab Nationalism and the Ottoman Caliphate', *Journal of Near Eastern Studies*, Vol. 71, No. 2 (2 October 2012), pp. 315–24.

[18] See further Bassam Tibi, *Arab Nationalism: Between Islam and the Nation-State*, New York: Palgrave Macmillan, 1997, p. 114.

[19] Quoted in William L. Cleveland, *The Making of an Arab Nationalist: Ottomanism and Arabism in the Life and Thought of Sati' al-Husri*, Princeton: Princeton University Press, 1971, p. 105, emphasis added.

language, which is geared to create an anatomy of his idea of an Arab superstate. In a final ideological stroke which links his psycho-nationalism to the idea of a nation-state, al-Husri says: 'When the language became the heart and spirit of the nation, then the people who spoke one language possessed one heart and a common spirit and therefore formed a nation. It then became necessary that they create one state'.[20] Ibn-Khaldun would have probably smiled at such a hysterical and anti-philosophical definition of a nation.

If Ibn Khaldun is one of the forerunners of the idea of community, then Ferdowsi must be recognised as one of the icons of the eastern belles-lettres. A supremely gifted poet, Ferdowsi finished the millennial book of kings in 1010 AD. Like Ibn Khaldun, Ferdowsi was concerned with society, politics, community, the rise and fall of empires, etc. But his method was different. Ibn Khaldun spoke as a social scientist; Ferdowsi used the language of romance. Accordingly, the Shahnameh charts the history of Persia from pre-Islamic kingdoms to the Muslim conquest in the seventh century AD. From the perspective of European Orientalists, this emphasis on Iran's pre-Islamic heritage and his interest in using Persian (Farsi) as a literary medium was indicative of Ferdowsi's aversion to Arabs and Islam in general.[21]

Orientalist themes played a major role in turning the shah-nameh into a psycho-nationalist trope for Iran's nascent dynasties in the nineteenth and twentieth century. Furthermore, Persian language journals such as *Kaveh* and *Iranshahr*, which were published in Berlin by a group of influential Iranian intellectuals with a nationalist conviction, presented Ferdowsi as an icon of a unique and distinctive Iranian national identity. In particular Hassan Taqizadeh (1878–1969), the veteran activist of Iran's Constitutional Revolt who edited *Kaveh* between 1916 and 22, superimposed western Orientalism on to the legacy of Ferdowsi. Highly influenced in his reading of Ferdowsi by

---

[20] Ibid., p. 105.
[21] See further Alireza Asgharzadeh, *Iran and the Challenge of Diversity: Islamic Fundamentalism, Aryanist Racism, and Democratic Struggles*, New York: Palgrave Macmillan, 2007.

Theodor Höldeke's (1836–1930) 'Das Iranische Nationalepos' (the Iranian national epic), Taqizadeh famously proclaimed that Iranians had to embrace everything European wholeheartedly.[22] It was this Europeanised Seyyed, in Iran's intellectual history, a lecturer at SOAS, University of London, among other prominent institutions, who was instrumental in inventing the shahnameh as a source of Iranian national identity.[23] In true psycho-nationalist parlance, Taqizadeh argued that Ferdowsi was the one who 'spun Iranian history and the national story into a perfectly structured narrative, and by establishing this narrative he has created one of the causes of glory for the Iranian nation and has preserved the national story until today'.[24] Taqizadeh uses a distinctly emotive and modern language in order to present the shahnameh as a source of a purified national pride and consciousness. In this way, he is a psycho-nationalist par excellence and he should be read and understood in conjunction with Fichte, Herder, Mazzini, von-Ranke and others.[25]

Undoubtedly, Ferdowsi was not indifferent to the politics of his day, not least because his livelihood was dependent on the patronage of the Ghaznavid court. As he concedes in the shahnameh itself: when the poet comes to the shah, 'he cannot choose but sit before the throne'. Comparable to the tracts of Ibn Khaldun, there is a lot in the shahnameh about the conduct in politics, community relations, humanity, governance, and identity centuries before scholars and poets in Western and Central Europe experimented with similar tropes. Yet it is central to my argument that the psycho-nationalist interpretations were superimposed. Neither Ibn Khaldun, nor Ferdowsi advocated worshipping the state and the nation. The hysterical emphasis on romance and love with reference to national

---

[22] See further Hamid Dabashi, *Post-Orientalism: Knowledge and Power in a Time of Terror*, London: Transaction Publishers, 2009.
[23] See further Afshin Marashi, *Nationalising Iran: Culture, Power, and the State, 1870–1940*, Seattle: University of Washington Press, 2008, pp. 123–25.
[24] *Kaveh*, 3rd October (new edition, no. 10), p. 12.
[25] Taqizadeh mingled with the 'Orientalists' of his day including A.J. Arberry and Walter Bruno Henning. He went on to chair several organisations in 'Iranian Studies'.

sentiments is a typically modern project. A global reading of such historical junctures demonstrates that eastern modernities produced their own pioneers of such psycho-nationalism. Iran is simply one example among many.[26]

Moreover, in Ferdowsi, the 'other' does not emerge as ultimately alien, discomforting and fundamentally different, as psycho-nationalists would have it. The shahnameh displays literary genius written in a cosmopolitan mode. The idea that the book presents a manifesto of purely Iranian origin, undiluted by the vicissitudes of history, and an ideological manifesto against everything non-Iranian is a modern fallacy. It is true that Ferdowsi glorified what he imagined to be Iranian culture, but the shahnameh is rather more of a cultural festival than an ideological phalanx pointed against the non-Iranian world. As Dick Davies rightly points out in his extensive research about this subject Ferdowsi also introduced what he considered to be non-Iranians who are portrayed in a positive light, such as women from all over Asia, in particular Sindokht, Rudabeh, Manizheh and Farigis. The only central female character who is portrayed in a negative light is Soudabeh, who is represented as the ultimate 'femme fatale' who tries to lie and cheat her way to her step-son Siyavash in order to seduce him. In accordance with the patriarchal reading of society characteristic of his period, Ferdowsi must have thought those rather bad character traits. The husband of Soudabeh, the King of Persia Kaykavoos, on the other side, is repeatedly portrayed as incompetent and reckless. In fact, all heroes of the shahnameh have a mixed lineage and are far from purely 'Iranian' or 'Aryan': the mother of the main protagonist, Rostam, is part Indian and part of demonic descent, and the mothers of the princes Siyavash and Esfandiyar come from Central Asia and Rum (the Christian West), respectively.

---

[26] See further, Jack Goody, *Renaissances: The One or the Many?* Cambridge: Cambridge University Press, 2010.

Divested of psycho-nationalist ideology, then, the shahnameh displays literal hybridity and aesthetic synergy rather than purity and difference. It narrates a 'society that embodies constant internal contradictions; that has an extremely porous rather than simply oppositional relationship with surrounding cultures'.[27] The shahnameh shows social life in its heterogeneous manifestations. 'If there is a unity to be found in these tales it is a unity of diversity, of *dis*unity . . . rather than of a single geographic area, or of a single bloodline, or of a single tribe . . . or of a single religious tradition'.[28] Persian culture, Hamid Dabashi recently wrote, is imbued with global thought and world culture.[29] Conversely, prominent doyens of 'Iranian Studies' such as Ehsan Yarshater are wrong to assume that 'Iranian identity is clearly asserted in the inscriptions of Darius the Great (522–486 B.C.) who as an Aryan and a Persian was fully conscious of his racial affiliation and proud of his national identity'.[30] It is problematic, typical and retroactive to assume that language carries identity, that Persian can ever be 'the chief carrier of the Persian world view and Persian cultures'.[31] Indeed, I would go one step further and add that imagining an 'original' Iran has been the cardinal sin of contemporary Iranian history. As we will continue to find out, several depictions of Iran (or 'Irans') have been invented in accordance with political currents. There is no original identity to Iran. Originality is the standard parody that psycho-nationalists routinely display, in Iran and elsewhere.

So the myths of a particularly Iranian or Persian identity were created within a historical context that was geared to psycho-nationalist currents, as demonstrated. Several studies have shown how in the twentieth century the shahnameh was reinvented as a source

---

[27] Dick Davies, 'Iran and Aniran', in Abbas Amanat and Farzin Vejdani (eds.), *Iran Facing Others: Identity Boundaries in a Historical Perspective*, London: Palgrave, 2012, pp. 46–7.
[28] Ibid. p. 47.
[29] See further: Hamid Dabashi, *The World of Persian Literary Humanism*, Cambridge: Harvard University Press, 2012.
[30] Ehsan Yarshater, 'Persian Identity in Historical Perspective', *Iranian Studies*, Vol. 26, No. 1–2, 2007, p. 141.
[31] Ibid. p. 142.

for Iran's psycho-nationalist project, which was intimately linked to imagining a nation ruled by a monarch represented by the Pahlavi dynasty. The shahnameh as a psycho-nationalist trope was meant to function for the Pahlavi monarchs in at least two ways: first, it was thought to be functional in linking their legitimacy to the emperors of pre-Islamic Persia, and second to emphasise Iran's difference to the 'Semitic' Arabs. From this perspective, Islam was deemed 'other' to Iran's 'true' identity which was invented as Aryan, closer to Europe, even France as the shah argued in 1963 in an article for *Life* magazine. Hence, a shahnameh 'industry' emerged in Iran in the 1920s and 1930s, institutionalised in educational curricula in Iranian schools after the first Pahlavi monarch assumed power in 1925. Subsequently, building on ideas developed by Taqizadeh in the aforementioned Berlin-based journals *Kaveh* and *Iranshahr*, Reza Shah sponsored the newly established Society for National Monuments (*anjoman-e asar-e melli*) to build a mausoleum for Ferdowsi in Tus, located in northeastern Iran.[32] The architecture of the mausoleum reflects its political utility: it was built in the Achaemenidian style perfectly in tune with the penchant of the Pahlavi dynasty for pre-Islamic Persian empires. Uniformity in discourse facilitated uniformity in culture, which subdued the mosaic, multicultural beauty of architectural designs in Iran. Furthermore, the *farvahar*, a Zoroastrian symbol central to the empire of Cyrus, satisfied the political quest to disassociate Iranian history and identity from Islam. Not entirely unlike the swastika which has been a prominent symbol in Hindu, Buddhist and Jainist religious folklore for millennia and which was then abused by the Nazis in Germany as a symbol for racial purity, the *farvahar* too travelled a long way from its neo-Assyrian habitat to Pahlavi Iran, where it was used as an emblem for Aryan/Persian purity.

[32] See further Afshin Marashi, 'The Nation's Poet: Ferdowsi and the Iranian National Imagination', in Touraj Atabaki (ed.), *Iran in the 20th Century: Historiography and Political Culture*, London: I.B. Tauris, 2009, pp. 93–111.

In a similar vein, reference to the mausoleum of Ferdowsi as the *ferdowsiyeh* was meant to reinvent the site as a destination for pilgrimage, in lieu of Shia-Islamic mausoleums that were traditionally called *hosseiniyeh*, itself a religious term invented by the Safavids, as we will find out at a later stage. In this way the public sphere in Iran became the carrier of a new form of theo-nationalistic indoctrination which was meant to signify a new kind of Persian purity. The dynamics, not at all reducible to the Iranian case as we have seen, were quintessentially psycho-nationalist: they were meant to cleanse the ideational archives from any impingement of the 'other' in order to simulate a false sense of authenticity and difference as opposed to a gratifying feeling of hybridity and multiculturalism which is closer to almost any social reality, certainly that of Iran. The fact that the engineers of such machoistic and ill-founded Persian pride worked at the nexus of power and knowledge, influential figures of the past such as Hassan Taqizadeh and Hassan Pirnya in Iran, or the army of Persian chauvinists outside of the country today, demonstrates the salience of this psycho-nationalist discourse. So deep runs Iranian psycho-nationalism, that leaders of the contemporary Iranian state, the Islamic Republic which at the beginning of the revolution was repulsed by the nationalistic innuendo of the Pahlavi dynasty, repeatedly reignited the country's pre-Islamic past as a source of identity. For instance, the former Iranian President Mahmoud Ahmadinejad praised the Cyrus cylinder when it was lent to Iran by the British Museum. In several statements, Ahmadinejad described Cyrus as an Iranian monarch who brought justice to the world 'look at Cyrus. He had taken over the whole world, but he said, "If anyone does anything unjust, he will have to come and face me." He said he would do everything within this Declaration of Rights'.[33] Ahmadinejad was quickly reprimanded by the clerical leadership who reminded him that Cyrus was not a Muslim and that he was a symbol of the Pahlavi monarchs. The Iranian state today is caught between such repeated

---

[33] Available at http://edition.presstv.ir/detail.fa/142906.html (accessed 3 January 2016).

bouts of Irano-centric psycho-nationalism and its Shia-Islamic corollary. Allow me to set a few signposts for the story of the latter.

ROSTAM ↔ HOSSEIN: SHIA MIND GAMES

The previous section developed my argument in two directions. Firstly, it showed that psycho-nationalism is a truly global phenomenon that has occurred in different regions at different periods of time and that it is analytically flawed to pinpoint a western origin to nationalist thinking. Secondly, it demonstrated how texts and ideas travel and how they develop into something very different in response to political necessity and/or ideological expediency. The shahnameh of Ferdowsi is a book of literary genius, a set of fables that are a testament to Persia's cosmopolitan heritage at the crossroads of cultures and ideas. Yet even this intricate mosaic of Iran's historical reality was shattered by psycho-nationalists from Taqizadeh and Kazimzadeh to Kermani and Akhundzadeh. It was then adopted by the Pahlavi dynasty, not as a trope to bring Iranians together in a civil, pluralistic, democratic nation-state, but to legitimate a new form of authoritarianism in the name of a Persianist ideal with racist undertones.

In order to put those dynamics into a global perspective the Pahlavis could have referred to the shahnameh in the same way that the Portuguese refer to their very comparable national epic today. For the Portuguese *Os Lusiadas* (The Lusiads in Portuguese), an epic poem authored by Luis Vaz de Camoes in the sixteenth century, which celebrates Portuguese discoveries in the East, has ceased to be a document for psycho-nationalist mobilisation. Like Ferdowsi, Camoes' poetry is embedded in a thick national repository which has been abused for ideological ends, exactly because of its folkloric stamina. Until today his death is celebrated as the national day of Portugal, yet without much nationalist hysteria anymore. This was different in the past when the same day served as a focal point for the dictatorship of Antonio Salazar (1889–1970). For instance in 1944, Salazar referred to the national day as the day of the 'Portuguese race'

(*Dia da Raça*), in close affinity with psycho-nationalist terminology.[34] For this dictatorship Camoes was as suitable to cognitive mind control as Ferdowsi was for the Pahlavi monarchy in Iran. At the same time, some countries, including Portugal at this point of history as a part of the European Union, have embraced a form of post-national politics that divests nationalised tropes and heritage of their aggressive identitarian punch and turns them into a carnival of positive emotions. This is politics after identity, if you like. Yet such consensual, non-confrontationist, agonistic approaches have not been implemented by successive Iranian states. Admittedly, the stakes have been higher than in the case of Portugal given Iran's sensitive geostrategic position in the Persian Gulf and the interference of foreign powers in the internal affairs of the country because of oil politics.[35] But this historical trajectory should not divert attention from the fact that contemporary Iran has been governed by a chauvinistic, hegemonic and rather hysterical and pathological form of politics which I have termed psycho-nationalist. Successive Iranian rulers have attempted to code the cognition of the populace along nefarious themes such as blood, honour and sacrifice – in the end rather unsuccessfully, as we will see.

Not all nationalism is antagonistic and hegemonic. An idea of Iran or any other nation that is imagined and institutionalised along flexible, inclusive and sufficiently complex signposts, that are as thinly ideational as possible, would minimise clashes in the name of identity. So-called 'historic' nations such as Iran, comparable to countries such as Russia, China, France, Japan and the United Kingdom and newer inventions such as the United States, seem to carry an identity complex. They repeatedly push, shove and bully the rest of us into believing in their historical mission which is recurrently the source

---

[34] See further https://jpn.up.pt/2004/06/09/estado-novo-10-de-junho-e-dia-da-raca/ (accessed 24 November 2016).

[35] For an excellent analysis of the Portuguese-Iranian interaction with reference to the island of Hormuz see Ghoncheh Tazmini, 'The Persian-Portuguese Encounter in Hormuz: Orientalism Reconsidered', *Iranian Studies*, Vol. 50, No. 2, 2017, pp. 271–92.

of anguish, pain and suffering on a global scale. Psycho-nationalism does to politics what terrorism does to society: it creates anxiety, angst, destructive emotions that appeal to the worst characteristics of human kind. In other words, psycho-nationalism creates a form of psychotic politics that is akin to terrorism.

In this section I will differentiate and open up the sites of psycho-nationalism further. The conventional literature of Iranian studies locates the emergence of the modern nation-state in the period of the Pahlavi dynasty, in particular the emergence of a nationalised infrastructure including banks, universities, citizenship and/or a national Iranian army under the leadership of Reza Shah who ruled Iran between 1925 and 41. Mainstream scholarship in Australia, Europe, North America and to a lesser extent East Asia and Latin America subscribes to this periodisation. As indicated above, nationalism is routinely analysed from a Eurocentric perspective and this view travels to other places around the world. Accordingly, nationalism in Iran is repeatedly represented as a historical trajectory rooted in European modernity. But as we have seen, such Eurocentric approaches to history overlook the circularity of ideas and the southern/eastern precedents to seemingly 'European' inventions. In this vein, I argue that the modern contours of the Iranian nation-state were created as early as the Safavid dynasty which ruled Iran between 1501 and 1722 (with a brief period of reappearance between 1729 and 36). I will add in a second step that the Safavids institutionalised the second prominent psycho-nationalist trope in the Iranian imagination, namely through a set of 'Shia paraphernalia'. Many of these devices to control Iranians continue to be central pillars of the contemporary Iranian state after the 'Islamic' revolution of 1979.

Ironically, the founder of the Safavid dynasty, Shah Ismail, was another product of the cosmopolitan and multicultural reality of Iran. He was born in 1487 to a sheikh of the Safaviyya Sufi order with Kurdish descent. His mother, Halima Begum, had Pontic Greek ancestors and Ismail himself was raised speaking both Persian and Azerbaijani (a Turkish dialect).[36] From their ancestral home in Ardabil, the Safavids expanded their rule to other parts of contemporary Iran and beyond. Between 1500 and 10, Shah Ismail incorporated Baghdad, Tabriz, Armenia, Azerbaijan, parts of Dagestan, Khorasan and Herat to the emerging empire. A gifted poet in his own right, the aesthetic culture sponsored by Shah Ismail was influenced by the shahnameh of Ferdowsi, which is one of the reasons why he named all of his sons after the characters of the book. It was Shah Ismail, then, who established the contours of Iran's contemporary nation-state long before the Treaty of Westphalia in 1648, which marked the end of the 30-year war and which is routinely given as the starting point for the emergence of modern nation-states in Europe. Moreover, it was he who used a very particularistic view of Persia as an anchor for his legitimacy. Hence, it should not come as a surprise that the shahnameh too was reinvented by Safavid court poets in order to function as a sub-narrative to the 'heroic' rule of Safavid monarchs. The Safavid dynasty understood the importance of (psycho)nationalist identity politics, long before the Pahlavis did (and the Europeans, as indicated).

But the 'myth of Persia' was not the only identity trope that was used by the Safavids to consolidate and expand their empire. When Shah Ismail came to power, contemporary Iran was populated mostly by Sunnis adhering to the Shafi'i and Hanafi legal schools. It must have appeared to him politically and ideologically prudent to differentiate his rule, not only in terms of national identity, but also with reference to God. After all, an earthly sovereignty and legitimacy is easily challenged, in particular because of the overwhelming presence of the Ottoman Empire and to a lesser extent successive Uzbek dynasties in Central Asia. The politics of identity, the antagonistic

---

[36] See further Roger M. Savory, 'Safavids' in Peter Burke, Irfan Habib, Halil İnalcık (eds.), *History of Humanity-Scientific and Cultural Development: From the Sixteenth to the Eighteenth Century*, Taylor & Francis, 1999, p. 259.

depiction of the 'other', became a major factor in the Safavid–Ottoman rivalry. The Ottomans were the heirs of the Islamic caliphate whose religious legitimacy was primarily based on Sunni traditions. In contrast, Shah Ismail pursued a relentless campaign of forced conversion of the majority Sunni population in Iran to (Twelver) Shia Islam. It is one of the many ironies of global history that before the ascendancy to power of the Safavid dynasty, the Ottomans routinely sent their Islamic scholars (*ulema*) to Iranian madrasas for their further education in Sunni jurisprudence (*fiqh*). From the perspective of Shah Ismail, the Safavid empire could only compete with the Ottomans if it were to institutionalise a strong state with a largely coherent and amalgamated nation, a subject citizenry that would accept the divine authority of the Shah who described himself as the reincarnation of Rostam, 'Jesus the Son of Mary' and Alexander.[37]

This process of subjectification was discursive and crude. Shah Ismail I administered what has been called an 'involuntary' and forced conversion policy, which was largely incomplete given that some areas under the domain of the Safavids retained their Sunni/Hanafi convictions.[38] But the discursive, psycho-nationalist strategies had long-term effects on the national imagination in Iran. Shah Ismail instituted an authoritarian regime over knowledge and power in the name of a missionary Shia ideology that was increasingly systematic and institutionalised.[39] Above all, this discursive regime targeted the cognition of the population through strident forms of biopolitical training and enforced socialisation into the Persianised Shia system. These methods included: reintroducing the office of the Sadr ('leader' in Arabic) which was responsible for supervising the burgeoning Shia mosque system in the empire and other religious

---

[37] Andrew J. Newman, *Safavid Iran: Rebirth of a Persian Empire*, London: I.B. Tauris, 2006, pp. 13–14.

[38] See further Rudi Matthee, *Persia in Crisis: Safavid Decline and the Fall of Isfahan*, London: I.B. Tauris, 2011, p. 174.

[39] See further Maryam Moazzen, 'Rituals of Commemoration, Rituals of Self-Invention: Safavid Religious Colleges, and the Collective Memory of the Shia', *Iranian Studies*, Vol. 49, No. 4, 2016, pp. 555–75.

sites and endowments; enforcing the ritual cursing of the first three Caliphs of the Sunna, that is, Abu Bakr, Umar and Osman; and inviting all the Shia living outside of the empire to come to Iran and to accept the Shah's sovereignty as the representative of the hidden Imam. According to Shia orthodoxy, this Imam Mahdi will return to earth (together with Jesus) to deliver the ideal human order. Some of these ideological tenets and the measures that derived from them were relaxed during the reign of Shah Ismail II (1537–77), but with the ascendancy to the throne of Shah Abbas I (1571–1629) they reappeared as a major pillar of Safavid state policy.

Secondly, Safavid psycho-nationalism was carried forward by an emerging caste of Shia clerics (*ulema*), who had arrived under sponsorship from Jabal Amil, Mount Lebaonon, Syria, Bahrain and Southern Iraq. From this point on, the clerical strata of society in Iran had the opportunity to engineer a new form of institutionalised Shi'ism, which gave them unprecedented access to the corridors of power, and does so until the present day. To that end, education was key. Psycho-nationalism, as I have conceptualised it, is galvanised by a strong nexus between power and knowledge, within a system that produces truth conditions on every level of the state and society in order to bind both together into the organisational outfit of the nation-state. As such, under the Safavids, and in particular during the rule of Shah Abbas I (1571–1629), the idea of Imamite jurisprudence in the Twelver-Shia tradition was institutionalised in the burgeoning *madrasas* and other educational and civic institutions sponsored by the court. These were increasingly populated by senior Shia scholars recruited from all over the Muslim world. Chief among them was Muhaqiq al-Karaki (also al-Thani, d. 1533), a pivotal clerical figure that readily carried the torch of the state-sponsored Shi'ism institutionalised during that period. In his widely disseminated study, *Refuting the Criminal Invectives of Mysticism (Mata'in al Mufrimiya fi Radd al-Sufiya)*, Al-Karaki established one of the most powerful refutations of the Sufi tradition in Iran and set the jurisprudential guidelines for the predominant authority of the jurist based on the

Imamite succession.[40] As a consequence, the *usuli* (rationalist) school of Shia Islam increasingly dominated the seminaries and pushed back the followers of the traditionalist (*akhbari*) paradigm. Al-Karaki and other influential clerics emphasised the power of *ijtihad* or dialectical reasoning and made a strong case in favour of the leadership of *mujtahids* whose divine decrees would be emulated (*taqlid*) by their followers.[41] As such, Al-Karaki's reinvention of a Shia orthodoxy based on a religious hierarchy dominated by a supreme jurist can be seen as one of the main precursors to Khomeini's idea of the *Velayat-e faqih* or the rule of the supreme jurisprudent.[42]

And thirdly, the Safavid discourse was carried into the heartland of the empire by a caste of men of the pen (*ahl-al qalam*), a highly educated, urban administrative class of society which maintained the humdrum affairs of the state. The individuals, trained in the ancient etiquette of *adab*, administered the financial, religious, political, ideological and diplomatic affairs of the Safavid court. These *adibs*, who were well-versed in ancient Greek philosophy and in the treatise of Farabi, Tusi, Sistani and Ibn Sina, used refined oratory skills and rhetoric as a socio-political strategy, a form of political ethics as a means to ordering society. In many ways the *adibs* were highly cultured managers of the public mind. They targeted the imagination (*khiyal*) of the Iranian population through discursive strategies such as *takhyil*, a particularly sophisticated form of socio-political argumentation through the use of figurative language and metaphors.[43]

---

[40] See Rula Jurdi Abisaab, *Converting Persia: Religion and Power in the Safavid Empire*, London: I.B. Tauris, 2004, p. 24. For Karaki's writings see Muhaqiq al-Karaki, *Jameal Maqasid*, Vol. 2, Qum: AhlolBayt Publication, 1365 [1986].

[41] See Mohammad Ali Amir-Moezzi, *The Divine Guide in Early Shi'ism: The Sources of Esotericism in Islam*, trans. David Streight, Albany: State University of New York Press, 1994, pp. 138–9.

[42] For a full history of the idea of *marjaiyat*, see Abdulaziz Abdulhussein Sachedina, *The Just Ruler in Shi'ite Islam: The Comprehensive Authority of the Jurist in Imamite Jurisprudence*, Oxford: Oxford University Press, 1998; see also Linda Walbridge, *The Most Learned of the Shi'a: The Institution of the Marja' Taqlid*, Oxford: Oxford University Press, 2001, in particular pp. 1–12.

[43] See further Julie Scott Meisami, *Structure and Meaning in Medieval Arabic and Persian Lyric Poetry: Orient Pearls*, London: Routledge, 2002.

In this way the *adibs* staged and narrated Safavid psycho-nationalism. Comparable to the role of humanists such as Erasmus or Cervantes in continental Europe, the *adibs* were the directors of an immensely rich politico-cultural theatre populated by metaphors, oratorical speeches, poetry, synonyms, norms and symbols. All of these oral and literary skills were useful in accessing the ancient archives (oral and written) of Iran's cultural and historical imagination, all the fables, books, philosophical tracts, parables, dictums and ideas that were invented to make up a 'Persian' or Iranian spirit. No wonder that the *adibs* found privileged employment in the chancelleries and other prominent institutions of the Safavid Court. Safavid mind games could only be effectively implemented with the help of this flamboyant stratum of society.

And lastly, even architectural styles are affected by the psycho-nationalism of the age. I have already indicated that the Pahlavis sponsored pre-Islamic styles for public buildings and cultural places such as the tomb of Ferdowsi. For instance, the National Museum of Iran, which was constructed from 1933 onwards, was built in the 'antiquarian Sassanid style'.[44] The Achaemenid style was used for buildings such as the National Bank, which was inaugurated in 1936, the Police Headquarters Building finished in 1934, the Darband Police Station inaugurated one year earlier and the Anoushiravan Dadgar High School in Tehran (1936). These buildings inscribed the obsession of the Pahlavis with pre-Islamic Persia, and their Aryan ideal, into the infrastructure of contemporary Iran. The imprint of the Safavids had equally important roots in the mechanisms of psycho-nationalism. The first generation of Safavid rulers (Ismail I, II and Tahmasp), in line with their newly acquired Shia persuasion, paid a lot of attention to restoring and extending major Shia shrines in Najaf, Karbala, Kazimiyya, Mashhad and elsewhere. Whereas the Ottomans (like the

---

[44] Kamran Safamanesh, 'Architectural Historiography, 1921–1942', in Touraj Atabaki (ed.), *Iran in the 20th Century: Historiography and Political Culture*, London: I.B. Tauris, p. 141.

Mughals in India) marked the expansion of their empire with the construction of magnificent Friday mosques, primarily in Istanbul, the imperial iconography of the Safavids was permeated by the Persian-Shia discourse underlying the claim to divine sovereignty of the shah.[45] This material portrayal of the Safavid 'self' culminated in the Shah mosque in Isfahan, which was completed in 1629. The universal claim was inscribed beautifully into the *maidan-e nakhshe jahan*, which translates quite aptly into the 'image of the world square'. The Persian proverb 'Isfahan is half of the world' (*Isfahan nesfeh jahan ast*) was coined during that period. The Safavid shahs did not only call themselves 'pivots of the universe', they endeavoured to inscribe their grand narratives onto the architectural fabric of Iran. This is to reiterate that architecture can be identified as another site of psycho-nationalist indoctrination, in Iran and elsewhere.

---

[45] See further, Kishwar Rizvi, *The Safavid Dynastic Shrine: Architecture, Religion and Power in Early Modern Iran*, London: I.B. Tauris, 2011, p. 3.

2 International Hubris: Kings of Kings and Vicegerents of God

I have argued that psycho-nationalism targets our cognition, our way of thinking about us and the community that we imagine as *our* nation. To that end, there exists a dense system of norms, institutions, bureaucracy and other machinations of the state that are intimately tied up in order to simulate the reality of 'us' which always also implies some form of aggression towards the 'other'. This overemphasis on the 'self' as a means to narrate the national community and its borders, begets a form of 'nationalistic narcissism'. In this way psycho-nationalism is not only played out as domestic politics. The nation-state is not merely something our politicians construct in their day-to-day interference in our daily lives. In fact, the nation-state is always also constructed in global politics.[1] Nationalistic narcissism gives impetus to a hubristic self-perception of the in-group, i.e. those that are considered to be a part of the nation. There is no better place than the international system to portray, enact and solidify such emotions. In other words: the international system is the place where the nation-state takes its 'selfies' and where it posts them to the rest of the world. In many ways, this global space can be described as the 'Instagram' of identity politics.

When successive US presidents recurrently claim to be the 'leader of the free world', they are communicating this message both to domestic constituencies and to other actors in the international system. Psycho-nationalism, is both an internal strategy and an external one. If domestic politics is the realm of psycho-nationalist mind games targeting the general populace, foreign policy is about

---

[1] See further James Mayall, *Nationalism and International Society*, Cambridge: Cambridge University Press, 1990.

imagining the place of a country among the community of nations. The international affairs of a country are about claiming a status, questions of dignity, identity, reputation, emotions and words. In the Iranian case, certainly in the periods covered in this book, foreign policy has always also been about imagining global grandeur. Contemporary Iranian leaders, more professionally since the reign of Reza Shah (1921–41), did not tend to limit the international relations of the country to issues of survival and a narrow understanding of the 'national interest'. Even in the absence of material resources justifying their self-perception, Iranian leaders have claimed and aspired to regional and global power. Hence they have routinely subscribed to an Iranocentric perception of the world that has repeatedly lent itself to political hubris. This is exemplified by imperial titles such as 'pivot of the universe', 'king of kings', 'light of the Aryans', for the country's royal dynasties and 'leader of the Islamic nation' (or *umma*), 'shadow of god', etc., after the Islamicised revolution of 1979. Indeed, the only contemporary leader of Iran who did not claim an otherworldly title was Mohammad Mossadegh, Iran's first democratically elected Prime Minister who was deposed by a CIA/MI6 led coup d'état in 1953. Before him it was the legendary Karim Khan of the Zand dynasty, who was the only dynastic sovereign in Iranian history to reject the title of *shah-in-shah* or king of kings, adopting the title 'representative of the people' instead. Karim Khan-e Zand (1705–79) is a worthy topic of the melodrama composed by the Italian composer Nicolo Gabrielli di Quercita entitled *L'assedio di Sciraz* (The siege of Shiraz), which was first performed at the La Scala theatre in Milan in 1840. My maternal familial lineage goes back to Karim Khan. And I came to London via a genealogical and geographic trajectory that encompasses Persia, Arabia, Iraq, Turkey, Lebanon, Germany and the United States. This diverse ideational space may serve as yet another example of the myths of coherence and cultural uniformity at the heart of hermetic notions of identity.

In this chapter, I take seriously the spectre of identity construction that underlies the performance of the nation in foreign policy.

To that end, I connect the 'will to international power' in Iran through the discourses constituting the contemporary foreign policy culture of the country with the hubristic drives of Iran's psycho-nationalist legacies. In a second concluding step, I will sketch the discrepancy between Iranian claims and external recognition of those claims, which will explain why none of the contemporary grand discourses delineating Iran's self-perception in world politics legitimated a hegemonic regional power position. I will try to show that the reason is not necessarily a lack of material resources, but the inability of the contemporary Iranian state to forge a foreign policy culture that is not dependent on psycho-nationalist definitions of Iranian 'identity'. Whether under the shah or the Islamic Republic, the idea of Iran as it has been invented by the state and its underbelly has not had universal appeal; it has remained entangled and trapped in the narrow realm of psycho-nationalist politics, Persian-centric under the shah and Islamist/Shia-specific under the Islamic Republic. None of these imaginations of the Iranian 'self' have been easily amenable to legitimating claims to regional or global power. In short, psycho-nationalism in Iran has hampered Iran's international appeal. This is my first step towards showing that psycho-nationalism engenders its own 'psycho-therapeutic' resistance.

THE FOREIGN POLICY CULTURE OF IRAN

We all have an idea about who we are. In turn, our sense of selfhood is heavily influenced by processes of socialisation, our family background, profession, sexuality (e.g. being homo- or transsexual), religion (e.g. being Catholic or a Sufi) or national narratives or a mixture of all of those. A comparable sense of selfhood, heightened and dramatised by a good dose of theatrical performance and fancy modes of symbolisation, is adopted by modern nation-states.[2] Political elites conceive, invent, perform and dramatise the national narrative

---

[2] For a sociological take see Jeffrey C. Alexander, *Performance and Power*, London: Polity Press, 2011.

through anthems, stamps, parades, national holidays, the media and so on.[3] States are adamant to tell the world and their populace who they are and what they represent, not least in order to legitimate their claim to rule. So when the Supreme Guide of Iran, Ayatollah Khamenei, speaks of the 'victory of the Islamic Revolution in Iran, under the able leadership of Imam Khomeini, a courageous and learned descendant of the prophet'; when he deems the revolution a 'watershed event in Islamic awakening in the entire world, especially in the countries of our region';[4] and when he proclaims all this at a major international conference on Palestine, he places Iran at the centre of the international politics of the region, the Israeli-Palestinian conflict and the Muslim world (itself a problematic invention of course).

This centred perception of Iran's role in the world has become a part of the self-understanding of the Islamic Republic, much in the same way as the United States claims to be the leader of the free world and allocates immense material and ideational resources to perform this role. Iran as well has spent billions in order to be considered a regional superpower, the leader of the Islamic world or the pivot of the world-wide revolution of the 'oppressed', as Ayatollah Khomeini put it in 1979. To enact this role, the Iranian polity disseminates ideational and material resources throughout the state and its underbelly, in particular powerful foundations such as the *Bonyad-e Mostafazan* (the foundation of the oppressed), which are tied into a vast institutional network engaged in social and cultural projects throughout the world. After the revolution, and in particular in the last decade, Iran has also built a gigantic, state-sponsored media conglomerate which offers 24-hour news and other programmes in all major languages.

---

[3] For a very recent analysis of the impact of social media in Iran see Babak Rahimi and David M. Faris, *Social Media in Iran: Politics and Society after 2009*, Albany: State University of New York Press, 2015.

[4] 'Address by the Eminent Leader of the Islamic Republic of Iran, Ayatollah Khamenei, on the occasion of International Conference on Palestinian Intifada, Tehran, April 24, 2001'. Available at www.radioislam.org/tehranconference/eng.htm (accessed 12 August 2013).

Such processes of self-construction of nation-states are at the heart of contemporary politics and no one remains unaffected by them.

When Ayatollah Khamenei states that 'since the victory of the Islamic Revolution, the colonial powers have been stepping up their attempts at fomenting discord and schism between the Shia and Sunni' and when he immediately adds in the same paragraph that 'over the past years, considering that the Islamic Republic of Iran has accomplished a noble objective and conquered a high summit, which is the awakening of the Islamic world, the arrogant powers have now a stronger motive for the creation of discord and division among Muslims', he is narrating a role of Iran in world politics according to which the foreign policy elites of the country are meant to act.[5] The same political process underlay President Obama's speeches, for instance, when he reproduces the idea of 'America' as a beacon of freedom, justice and equality. These are not merely words, free-floating ideas without sturdy hinges. They are institutionalised; they permeate sophisticated ideational regimes of truth with a material base that carries the ideas forward and gives them objective 'reality'. This is what I meant by the term 'foreign policy culture' when I first introduced it in 2005.[6]

I have conceptualised foreign policy culture more in-depth in an article for *Middle East Critique*, a rather post-structural piece that presents methods and theories with reference to Iranian politics. Suffice it to say here, it is analytically important to acknowledge that the idea or a self-perception comes first, that it precedes the implementation of foreign policies and the interpretation of the 'national interest'. In the Iranian case the idea of being the centre of the Islamic world, or indeed the Third World, was crafted during the revolution.

---

[5] 'Leader's address to the participants in the 2nd congress in commemoration of Ibn Maytham Bahrani'. Available at www.leader.ir/en/speech/3588/Leader%E2%80%99s-Address-to-the-Participants-in-the-2nd-Congress-in-Commemoration-of-Ibn-Maytham-Bahrani (accessed 3 January 2017).

[6] See Arshin Adib-Moghaddam, 'Islamic Utopian Romanticism and the Foreign Policy Culture of Iran', *Middle East Critique*, Vol. 14, No. 3 (2005), pp. 265–92.

Khomeini repeatedly spoke in momentous terms when he referred to the revolution in Iran and its desired impact beyond the country. Speaking in March 1980, he reiterated in typically cosmic fashion:

> Know well that the world today belongs to the oppressed, and sooner or later they will triumph. They will inherit the earth and build the government of God. Once again, I declare my support for all the movements and groups that are fighting to gain liberation from the superpowers of the left and the right. I declare my support for the people of Occupied Palestine and Lebanon. I vehemently condemn once more the savage occupation of Afghanistan ... I hope that the noble Muslim people of Afghanistan will achieve victory and true independence as soon as possible, and be delivered from the clutches of the so-called champions of the working class.[7]

In a sophisticated process galvanising the construction of the post-revolutionary Iranian state identity, this self-perception became a salient norm, an institutionalised regime of truth, a discourse termed *sudur-e enghelab* (export of the revolution) in the first decade of the Islamic Republic, a constitutive part of Iran's foreign policy culture. It is in this way that foreign policy culture refers to the socially constructed perception of elites who are involved in the foreign policy-making process of a particular country. To put it in more formal terms: foreign policy culture refers to an integrated system of symbols (metaphors, analogies, imageries, languages, ideologies, norms, institutions, etc.) which act to define pervasive and embedded grand strategic preferences, based on the processing of indigenous and exogenous socialisation, affecting the mental disposition of agents vis-à-vis their environment and giving content to the interest to be pursued. The concept of foreign policy culture thus appreciates that

---

[7] Rouhollah Khomeini, *Islam and Revolution: Writings and Declarations of Imam Khomeini (1941–1980)*, edited and translated by Hamid Algar, Berkeley: Mizan Press, 1981, p. 287.

different countries approach the key issue of war, peace and strategy from deeply embedded perspectives that are intrinsic to the distinct political cultures of the agent(s). And to put it simply: by determining the perception of decision-makers, a particular foreign policy culture shapes the broad contours of a country's foreign policy agenda, defined in terms of grand strategic preferences.[8]

But the process of self-designation is not enough. If I would run around the SOAS campus and proclaim that I am Napoleon Bonaparte, I would have a hard time persuading anyone sane. At best, I would be the object of amusement; at worse I would be restrained. Self-designations as the leader of the free world or the pivot of Islam require external recognition in order to function efficiently. As I have argued elsewhere with regard to the international politics of the Persian Gulf, role identities neither are solitary inventions, nor can be enacted in isolation.[9] Any type of identity is dependent on processes of social engineering. In other words, if Iran wants to be acknowledged as the leader of the Islamic world, it has to be recognised as such by powerful elements of international society, which may explain why the Iranian state is spending so much money on public relations with the Muslim world in the first place. Yet as we will see in the next section, neither during the period of the shah, nor after the Islamic revolution of 1979, did Iran receive the external recognition of its self-proclaimed role as a regional/global power. Until today, the grandeur that Iranian leaders have sought (and the psycho-nationalist tropes that they have dedicated to that end) has been repeatedly frustrated.

BLIND SPOTS IN THE LIGHT OF THE ARYANS

If foreign policy is about aspiring to global grandeur, contemporary Iranian leaders have had a vivid imagination about the place of Iran in the world. Whether before the revolution of 1979 under the regime

---

[8] See further Adib-Moghaddam, 'Islamic Utopian Romanticism'.
[9] See Adib-Moghaddam, *The International Politics of the Persian Gulf*.

of the Pahlavi Shahs or under the Islamic Republic, the idea of Iran as a regional, if not global power, has been central to the foreign policy discourse of the political elites in the country. Certainly, Iran carries the burden of history in that regard, an imperial complex informed by the ancient history associated with the territory that is today's Iran. This imperial complex was particularly pronounced in the ideational constructs that were meant to legitimate the policies of shah Mohammad Reza Pahlavi and his father Reza Khan, as indicated in the past chapters. For the Pahlavi monarchs, the meaning of the country was primarily geared to the pre-Islamic Persian empires rather than to Islam, which they deemed alien to the 'true' and 'authentic' Iranian identity. I have called these forms of ideational manipulation psycho-nationalist because they target the very fabric of a nation's historical consciousness and sense of being. As such, they are weapons of mass deception.[10]

Exemplifying the psycho-nationalist politics of modern Iran, the first monarch of the short-lived Pahlavi dynasty, Reza Khan, invested immense resources into reconstructing the meaning of Iran along racialised notions of Aryanism. Based on that mythology, the Iranian foreign ministry disseminated a memo in 1934 according to which the name Iran (land of the Aryans) would substitute Persia in all international correspondence. The term 'Persia' was deemed an invention of the ancient Greeks who had invaded Iran and raided what they called 'Persepolis' or the city of the Persians. Ironically, then, it was the ancient Greeks who were instrumental in the decision of the shah to rename the country Iran. According to the memo, 'because Iran was the birthplace and origin of Aryans, it is natural that we should want to take advantage of this name, particularly since these days in the great nations of the world noise [sic] has gotten out regarding the Aryan race which indicates the greatness of the race and civilisation of ancient Iran'.[11]

---

[10] See further Adib-Moghaddam, *On the Arab Revolts and the Iranian Revolution*.
[11] Quoted in Firoozeh Kashani-Sabet, *Frontier Fictions*, p. 218.

This Aryan-centric discourse yielded and rationalised pro-Nazi policies which would eventually be used as a pretext to the invasion of Iran by allied forces in 1941. In the imagination of many Iranian writers during that period, the country was among the superior nations of the world. Reza Khan himself was presented as a charismatic leader comparable Mussolini and Hitler.[12] Journals such as *Nameh-ye Iran-e Bastan* (The Journal of Ancient Iran) experimented with racist ideas adopted from the cod science of the Nazis. They were rather forthcoming in their infatuation with Hitler whom they deemed 'a great scholarly man of the Aryan race'.[13] Moreover, the swastika was reinvented as an authentically Iranian symbol. 'It is truly rejoicing to see', it is noted in all sincerity, that the 'symbol of Iran from 2000 years before Christ has today become a symbol of pride for the Germans, who are of one race and ethnicity with us.'[14] The myth of racial affinity with the supposedly 'Aryan Germans' was fortified by a Nazi decree in 1936 which identified Iranians as 'pure blooded Aryans' thus exempting them from the Nuremburg Race Laws. Inspired by phrenological 'research' in Europe, the newly created Society for National Heritage even went so far as to dig up bodies in Ferdows, the birthplace of Ferdowsi whose shahnameh has been hailed by Iranian psycho-nationalist as an emblem of the purity of the Iranian language as discussed, in order to measure their skulls which would 'prove' their Aryan origin.[15] As a part of this psycho-nationalist reconstitution of the meaning of Iran, there emerged a policy of cultural purification which was aimed at eliminating Arabic words, and their 'Semitic' origins, from the Persian language. Prominent writers such as Ahmad Kasravi (1890–1946) were supportive of such measures, which were filtered through dedicated institutions such as

---

[12] See further Miron Rezun, M. *The Iranian Crisis of 1941: The Actors, Britain, Germany, and the Soviet Union*, Wien: Böhlau, 1982, p. 29.
[13] *Nameh-ye Iran-e Bastan*, August 1933, Issue 28, p. 1.
[14] Ibid.
[15] See also Ervand Abrahamian, *A History of Modern Iran*, Cambridge: Cambridge University Press, 2008, p. 87.

the *Farhangistan*. In summary then, Reza Shah imagined grandeur exactly in psycho-nationalist terms: Iranian identity was racialised and Iranian superiority was thus inscribed in the syntax of the emerging Pahlavian national narrative which was meant to signify a new meaning of the country.

Mohammad Reza Shah, the second and last monarch of the Pahlavi dynasty, was equally inspired by the discourse of Aryanism and the pre-Islamic Persian empires. He adopted the title 'light of the Aryans' (*Aryamehr*) and in his speeches and writings he repeatedly invoked the symbols and imagery of ancient Persia, the memory of Darius, Cyrus and Xerxes. At the height of his megalomania, exemplified by his Napoleon-esque self-coronation in 1967 and the extravagant festivities at Persepolis in 1971, the shah changed the Islamic solar hegra calendar into an imperial one. At the ancient seat of the Persian monarchs he invoked the spirit of Cyrus and placed his dynasty in line with the Achaemenidian kings of antiquity. In the opening speech of the festivities at Persepolis on 12 October 1971 he declared: 'O Cyrus, great King, King of Kings, Achaemenian King, King of the land of Iran. I, the Shahanshah of Iran, offer thee salutations from myself and from my nation. Rest in peace, for we are awake, and we will always stay awake.' The historical reengineering of the meaning of Iran is evident here. Suddenly, Iran was in the year 2535 based on the presumed date of the foundation of the Achaemenidian dynasty. In lieu with the effort to Iranianise the Persian language, which already had been pursued by his father Reza Khan, the Pahlavi state also sponsored systematic efforts to substitute Arabic terms with Persian ones.

The ideational architecture of 'Pahlavism' was crafted around the symbolism of monarchic rule and the metaphysics of modern (psycho)nationalism consisting of romantic myths about the authenticity of the 'Persian' language and the unique 'Iranian civilisation'. Their impact on the making of a modern 'identity' of Iran devoid of an intrinsically 'Islamic' component comes out in an article which the shah placed in *Life* magazine in May 1963: 'Geographically Iran is situated at the crossroads of the East and the West; it is where Asia and Europe meet,' the shah asserts. 'On one side thrived the old civilisations of China and India; on the other those of Egypt, Babylon, Greece, Rome, and, later on, the modern Western World.' His country was not a part of any civilisation per se, but 'Iran welded her own civilisation from all those many sources.' This distinctly Iranian civilisation holds a universal religion and universal art which 'have left their traces all over the world'. But this universal religion that the shah refers to is not conceptualised as Islamic. Rather, he heralds the pre-Islamic era, 'the old Iranian religion of Mithra' and the 'teachings of the mystic prophet Mani'.[16] So an Islam did not have much of a role in the making of an Iran during this period. A systematic discourse of Islam re-enters the re-imagination of what it means to be Iranian in the counter-culture of the 1960s and 1970s and after the Islamicised revolution of 1979.

The subject that emerges out of the shah's psycho-nationalist discourse is the Aryan Persian, Indo-European, heir to a lost civilisation but willing to catch up along an imagined western temporality (or historical spectrum). The shah repeatedly stressed that the culture of Iran was 'more akin to that of the West'. The country was deemed 'an early home of the Aryans from whom most Americans and Europeans are descended'. Racially, Iranians were considered to be 'quite separate from the Semitic stock of the Arabs'. As such, Iran was deemed to be the 'oldest culture that was racially and linguistically linked to the West'. After all, Persian 'belongs to the Indo-European family which includes English, German, and other major Western tongues [sic]'.[17] Elsewhere the shah stated that Iran was an 'Asian Aryan power whose mentality and philosophy are close to those of the European states, above all France'.[18] Along with that emphasis on

[16] Mohammad Reza Shah Pahlavi, 'A Future to Outshine Ancient Glories,' *Life*, 31 May 1963, p. 66.
[17] Mohammad Reza Pahlavi, *Mission for My Country*, New York: McGraw-Hill, 1961, p. 18.
[18] Quoted in Mangol Bayat-Philipp, 'A Phoenix Too Frequent: Historical Continuity in Modern Iranian Thought', *Asian and African Studies*, Vol. 12 (1978), p. 211.

Iran's western heritage went an imperial narrative: 'If you Europeans think yourselves superior, we have no complexes,' the shah emphasised in an interview with the flamboyant Italian journalist, Oriana Fallaci. 'Don't ever forget that whatever you have, we [pre-Islamic, 'Aryan' Iran] taught you three thousand years ago.'[19]

SIGNS OF GOD, ISLAMIST DEAD ENDS

It should by now have become clearer what I mean by psycho-nationalist fabrications. They target identity exactly. Moreover, they have been at the heart of modern politics because contemporary nation-states require some form of ideational content in order to sustain the rule of the sovereign: if Iran was Aryan, then the light of the Aryans is entitled to rule. If the meaning of Iran was encapsulated in the history of pre-Islamic Persia, then the shah-in-shah was the legitimate heir to Persia's ancient monarchies. If Iran had an imperial legacy, then the shah had the prerogative to pursue hegemonic foreign policies. Psycho-nationalism affords any state such causal power.

Before the revolution in 1979, a new discourse precipitated the psycho-nationalist reengineering of the meaning of Iran. In the most influential writings of Iran's prototypical revolutionary intellectuals, such as Jalal al-e Ahmad and Ali Shariati, Iranian history in particular and Islam in general were rewritten to function as building blocks for a viable revolutionary movement that was quite overtly and explicitly targeting the monarchy of the shah. So for al-e Ahmad, the rather laid back thirteenth century astronomer and philosopher Nasir ad-Din Tusi (1201-4) becomes the prototypical 'aggressive intellectual' (rowshanfekr-e mohajem), 'who made history' after obliterating the prevalent order seeking to 'destroy the contemporary governmental institutions in order to erect something better in their place'.[20] Whereas in Shariati, we find a comparable signification

---

[19] Oriana Fallaci, *Interview with History*, New York: Houghton-Mifflin, 1977, p. 264.
[20] Quoted in Anja Pistor-Hatam, 'Writing Back? Jalal Al-e Ahmad's (1923–69) Reflections on Selected Periods of Iranian history', *Iranian Studies*, Vol. 40, No. 5 (December 2007), p. 565.

of revolutionary change which is likened to a 'golden age of justice', a classless society, social equality and the final victory of the 'oppressed' masses against their 'oppressors'. Influenced by Marxist teleology, Shariati professed that there was no choice towards that end since the victory of the revolution was historically determined. This would make it mandatory for the vanguard to 'object to the status quo and to negate the ruling systems and values'.[21] With al-e Ahmad and Shariati, an entirely new ontology for Iran is imagined and increasingly enacted.

This newly imagined Iran was not provincial, as some scholars have argued. This revolutionary subject in Iran was not confined to a nativist habitat, even if it indulged in the utopia of 'authenticity'.[22] In the writings of intellectuals such as al-e Ahmad and Shariati we hear echoes of – and see direct reference to – Che Guevera, Marx, Sartre, Marcuse, Fanon and others. After all, this radical culture of resistance was also inscribed in the very linguistic infrastructure of Iran's capital Tehran after the revolution where major streets, boulevards and squares were named Bobby Sands, Gandhi, Africa and Palestine.[23] Al-e Ahmad and Shariati may have promoted radical politics to battle with the dictatorship of the Shah, but they were not fanatics. Their utopia was based on a rather more inclusive and democratic order in Iran in contrast to the Khomeinists who would perfect psycho-nationalism as a tool to rule the country.

---

[21] Quoted in Ali Rahnema, *An Islamic Utopian: A Political Biography of Ali Shariati*, London: I.B. Tauris, 2000, p. 305.

[22] There is emphasis on nativism in Mehrzad Boroujerdi, *Iranian Intellectuals and the West: The Tormented Triumph of Nativism*, Syracuse: Syracuse University Press, 1996.

[23] Bobby Sands street is located along the UK embassy in Tehran. In 1981, the Iranian government was officially represented at Bobby Sands' funeral and presented to Mrs. Sands a plaque honouring his activism. The Tehran city council also renamed a street in Tehran after Khaled Eslambouli who assassinated the former Egyptian President Anwar Sadat, although the Iranian foreign ministry has repeatedly tried to amend the name. In 2011, the city council decided to rename a street in central Tehran Rachel Aliene Corrie street, after the US American pro-Palestinian activist who was killed while protesting against the demolition of Palestinian homes in the Gaza strip eight years ago. It's the first time since Iran's Islamic Revolution in 1979 that an Iranian street had been named after a citizen of the United States.

Despite the obvious tilt to Islam as a liberation theology, it is in Shariati especially where east meets west on an immensely innovative critical spectrum, and where the potentialities of a seemingly contradictory 'Islamo-socialist' discourse are exploited in order to channel what was considered to be the emancipating message of Islam and socialism to receptive constituencies within Iranian society. This internationalist cross-fertilisation was not limited only to the intellectual/theoretical realm. For instance, the nascent Iranian armed movements of the 1960s drew their inspiration from theories of guerrilla warfare developed in Cuba, Nicaragua, Vietnam, Palestine and China.

As indicated, the social engineering of Iran's post-revolutionary identity discourse was precipitated and seriously affected by the writings of activist intellectuals whose ideas were widely disseminated among the anti-shah intelligentsia, especially in the late 1960s and 1970s. Two narratives, *gharbzadegi* (or westtoxification) and *bazgasht be khish* (return to the self), were particularly hegemonic. The former was the title of a highly influential book authored by al-e Ahmad. In this book he likens the increasing dependence of Iran on western notions of modernity to a disease he terms *gharbzadegi*. He picked up the term from Ahmad Fardid, an ardent Heideggerian philosopher who supported the revolution of 1979.[24] If left untreated *gharbzadegi* would lead to the demise of Iran's cultural, political and economic independence, because society was made susceptible to penetration by the West. 'Today', writes al-Ahmad, 'the fate of those two old rivals is, as you see, this: one has become a lowly groundskeeper and the other the owner of the ballpark.'[25] In order to escape this fate, al-e Ahmad argued, Iran had to be turned into the vanguard in the fight of the oppressed 'east' against the imperialist 'west', if necessary through revolutionary action.

[24] See further Ali Mirsepassi, *Transnationalism in Iranian Political Thought: The Life and Times of Ahmad Fardid* (The Global Middle East), Cambridge: Cambridge University Press, 2017.
[25] Jalal Al-e Ahmad, *Plagued by the West (Gharbzadegi)*, trans. Paul Sprachman, New York: Caravan, 1982, p. 19.

Shariati was equally adamant to challenge the policies of the shah and his real and perceived dependence on the politics of the United States. The narrative of *bazgasht be khish* picked up al-e Ahmad's theme accentuating cultural authenticity, and the wider anti-colonial struggle at the head of which Iran should position itself, not least in order to find a way back to the country's 'true' self which Shariati defined in socialist and Islamic terms. In an intellectual tour de force, Shariati turned Jesus, Abraham, Mohammad and above all Imam Hussein (grandson of the Prophet Muhammad) and his mother Fatimah into revolutionary heroes who were positioned at the helm of a new movement for global justice and equality. In his many speeches and written tracts, Shariati emphasised that Islam in general and Shia Islam, in particular, demands revolting against unjust rulers. At the centre of Shariati's oeuvre we find Imam Hussein who is represented as the ultimate *homo Islamicus*, a martyr in the cause of justice who fought the 'tyranny' of the Ummayad caliph Yazid and who sacrificed his life and that of his family at the Battle of Karbala in 680 AD. 'Look at Husayn!' Shariati demands in 1970.

> He is an unarmed, powerless and lonely man. But he is still responsible for the *jihad* . . . He who has no arms and no means has come with all of his existence, his family, his dearest companions so that his *shahadat* [bearing witness to God, martyrdom] and that of his whole family will bear witness to the fact that he carried out his responsibility at a time when truth was defenceless and unarmed . . . It is in this way that the dying of a human being guarantees the life of a nation. His *shahadat* is a means whereby faith can remain. It bears witness to the fact that great crimes, deception, oppression and tyranny rule. It proves that truth is being denied. It reveals the existence of values which are destroyed and forgotten. It is a red protest against a black sovereignty. It is a shout of anger in the silence which has cut off tongues.[26]

[26] Ali Shariati, 'On Martyrdom (*Shahadat*)', in John J. Donohue and John L. Esposito (eds.), *Islam in Transition: Muslim Perspectives*, 2nd edition, Oxford: Oxford University Press, 2007, p. 364.

The narratives of *gharbzadegi* and *bazgasht be khish* simulate a bifurcated syntactical order: justice ↔ oppressed (*mostazafan*) ↔ Muslim ↔ Islam ↔ revolution ↔ resistance *versus* imperialism ↔ oppressors (*mostakbaran*) ↔ superpowers ↔ the West ↔ the United States. Yet while Shariati and al-e Ahmad introduced, reinforced and gave impetus to the politics of identity and emotions in Iran's contemporary political culture, they were not vicious revolutionaries who were interested in power. If anything they were melancholic armchair thinkers, who wanted revolution for the sake of a rather more democratic and pluralistic political system.

In the writings and speeches of Ayatollah Khomeini, the dichotomies that opened up after the revolution of 1978/79 find their *explicit* psycho-nationalist articulation because they are infused with the will to power that he expressed from the outset. In his first speech after his return from exile, Khomeini made it clear that he would not compromise with the remnants of the government of the shah who had departed the country:

> This government represents a regime, whose leader and his father were illegally in power. This government is therefore illegal. The deputies appointed to work in the Majlis are there illegally. The Majlis itself and the Senate are illegal. How can anyone appointed by the shah be legal? We are telling all of them that they are illegal and they should go. We hereby announce that this government, which has presented itself as a legal government is in fact illegal. Even the members of this government before accepting to be ministers, were considering the whole establishment to be illegal. What has happened now, that they are claiming to be legitimate? This gentleman, Dr Bakhtiar [last Prime Minister of the shah] does not accept himself, and his friends do not accept him either. The nation does not accept him and the army does not accept him. Only America is backing him and has ordered the army to support him. Britain has backed him too and had said that he must be supported. If one were to search among the nation, one would not find a single

person among all strata of the nation who accepts this man, but he is saying that one country cannot have two governments. Well of course, it is clear that this country does not have two governments and in any case, the illegal government should go. You are illegal. The government of our choice relies on the nation's backing and enjoys the backing of God. If you claim that your government is legal, you must necessarily be denying God and the will of the nation. Someone must put this man in his place.[27]

The psycho-nationalist themes are apparent here: Khomeini puts particular emphasis on justice, national mobilisation against external and internal enemies and the politics of identity in the name of God and power. He is neatly delineating, quite from the outset, self and other, ally and enemy. Gone are the agonistic prescriptions in the name of freedom that were references in the writings and lectures of Shariati and al-e Ahmad who rejected any clerical leadership as reactionary and retroactive. Instead, Khomeini creates a new leviathan, the *vali-e faqih*, the supreme jurisprudent who would position himself at the helm of a global movement. Hence his emphasis on legitimacy, sovereignty and the will of god. Comparable to the other psycho-nationalist discourses studied in this book, Khomeini was first and foremost interested in fortifying the sovereignty and legitimacy of the (nation)-state which would have the prerogative to be a pan-Islamic example for the Muslim world – Iran came first. This was a truly modernist tactic. So while the shah proclaimed Iran's new civilisation based on the country's pre-Islamic heritage, a different meaning of Iran was being formulated – a discourse that produced another variant of psycho-nationalism in Iran, this time with a theocratic propeller. In this discourse, new 'others' emerge, certainly the 'west' in terms of the foreign relations of the country and a wide range of internal 'threats', for instance, religious and sexual minorities such as Bahais and homosexuals. Even in exile in Najaf, the discourse of

[27] Available at www.bbc.com/persian/revolution/khomeini.shtml (accessed 12 December 2016).

Khomeini was infused with this will to power that was so symptomatic of his political tactics.

'[T]he imperialists and the tyrannical self-seeking rulers have divided the Islamic homeland', Khomeini lectured in Najaf (Iraq) in 1970.

> They have separated the various segments of the Islamic umma from each other and artificially created separate nations. There once existed the great Ottoman State, and that, too, the imperialists divided ... In order to assure the unity of the Islamic *umma*, in order to liberate the Islamic homeland from occupation and penetration by the imperialists and their puppet governments, it is imperative that we establish a government. In order to attain the unity and freedom of the Muslim peoples, we must overthrow the oppressive governments installed by the imperialists and bring into existence an Islamic government of justice that will be in the service of the people. The formation of such a government will serve to preserve the disciplined unity of the Muslims; just as Fatima az-Zahra (upon whom be peace) said in her address: The Imamate exists for the sake of preserving order among the Muslims and replacing their disunity with unity.[28]

In this way, psycho-nationalism in Iran was being populated by new symbols and signs. Suddenly, the same people who were represented as heirs to the pre-Islamic Persian empires, as Aryan, Indo-European, even French and largely non-Muslim by the Pahlavis, appeared as primarily Islamic, anti-imperialistic, revolutionary and supportive of the struggles of the 'third worlds'. The occupation of the US embassy in 1979 was the practical epitome of this discourse. It was not merely planned in response to the admittance of the shah to the United States for medical treatment, which was interpreted as the beginning of yet another plot to reinstate his rule in Iran. The self-proclaimed

---

[28] Ruhollah Khomeini, *Islam and Revolution: Writings and Declarations of Imam Khomeini*, trans. and annotated by Hamid Algar, Berkeley: Mizan Press, 1981, pp. 48–9.

'students following the line of Imam Khomeini' were driven by ideas, coded by the powerful revolutionary narratives, some of which I have sketched above. As Masoumeh Ebtekar, one of the female students who was involved in the occupation of the US embassy, writes in her account of the events: 'My sense of women's rights and responsibilities derived much from the Iranian context, from Dr. Shariati's book *Fatima is Fatima*, in which he describes the Muslim woman and her role in the world of today with a mixture of eloquence and penetrating insight.'[29] Note that Fatima, conceptualised as the ultimate female vanguard of the new order, reappears here. She travelled from seventh century Arabia to claim a presence in the writings of Shariati (see above) and in the very consciousness of the revolutionaries. More strategically, the students deemed the occupation of the US embassy a necessary step towards achieving Iran's full independence from the international system, even if that meant that Iran would be labelled a pariah or rogue state by its most potent guardians. In other words, the choice to try to detach Iran from that system, which was deemed corrupt and geared towards the imperial interests of the superpowers, was self-consciously made by the more radical forces that gathered around Ayatollah Khomeini. As Ebtekar imagines: 'the Islamic Revolution in Iran transformed a once devoted ally of the west into a "rogue state" that insisted on taking orders from none other than God'.[30] The hubristic undertones should be evident here. Psycho-nationalism in Iran came full cycle with the triumph of the Khomeinist factions among the revolutionary forces.

IRANIAN POWER BETWEEN HUBRIS AND REALITY

The claims of political actors and their reception are different matters. Both before and after the revolution, Iran was never really accepted as a regional leader or a nodal point that could safeguard regional

---

[29] Massoumeh Ebtekar, *Takeover in Tehran: The Inside Story of the 1979 U.S. Embassy Capture*, Vancouver: Talon, 2000, p. 80.
[30] Ibid., p. 241.

security and progress. The Iranian state failed to forge an identity for the state that would have been inclusive enough to appeal to the major stakeholders in the region and beyond. From the perspective of regional leaders, and even the United States, the shah's self-centred ideology was suspect to say the least. As a CIA report, dated May 1972, indicated with increasing worry for the stability of the regime: 'Power in Iran remains, as it has been, in the hands of a small segment of society who enjoy the available rewards of money, status, and political influence . . . The shah sees himself in the role of a latter-day Cyrus the Great who will restore to Iran at least a portion of its old glory as a power to be reckoned with . . . A noncharismatic leader, he has taken on many of the trappings of totalitarianism.'[31]

From the perspective of the United States, the shah was a convenient and largely subservient regional ally, but there was no suggestion, implicit or otherwise, that Iran would be accepted as a regional power in its own right. Moreover, translated into the external relations of Pahlavi Iran, the self-identification of the country as an 'Aryan superpower' was anathema to an accepted leadership role in the region. In line with the notion of Iranian superiority, there emerged an aggressive military build-up under the patronage of the United States and to a lesser extent Israel, claims to Bahrain that were dropped only after a plebiscite in the small sheikhdom voted against unification with Iran, the seizure of half of the Abu Musa island from Sharjah, the Greater and Lesser Tunbs from Ras al-Khaimah in 1971, the decisive involvement of the shah's imperial army in the suppression of the Dhofar Marxist rebellion in Oman between 1973 and 4 and the sponsorship of Kurdish separatist forces in Northern Iraq in the late 1960s and early 1970s, in collusion with Israel and the United States. This brand of psycho-nationalism espoused by the shah and the foreign policy narratives and actions that it informed were so Irano-specific that they

---

[31] CIA, Directorate of Intelligence, 1972. *Intelligence Report: Centres of Power in Iran.* Available at: http://2001-2009.state.gov/documents/organization/70712.pdf (accessed 10 September 2013), pp. 1 and 11.

could never have acted as ideational devices to legitimate the country's claim to regional leadership and global grandeur.

The identity politics of the Islamic Republic after the revolution of 1979 were comparably exclusionary and ambitious, exclaiming as they continue to do, a regional, if not global leadership role. If Iran was the pivot of revolutionary Islam, the logic goes, then the sign of god (Ayatollah) was obliged to lead the nation. If the country re-enacts the original glory of the *ummah*, then following the Imam was a duty for all Muslims. Psycho-nationalism in the Islamic Republic attempts to invent the country as the vanguard of Islam and the legitimate leader of the 'Muslim nation'. As part of that effort and in order to avoid isolation of the revolution as a primarily Iranian event, the Islamic Republic has tried, largely unsuccessfully so far, to narrow the gap between the two areas of potential ideational contention, namely the Iranian-Arab and Sunni-Shia schisms. Such a decisive 'ecumenical' effort could not be implemented so far because psycho-nationalist tropes after the revolution in a Shia-Islamic garb continue to be promoted. There continues to be a feeling in Iran that the country is somehow entitled to grandeur. In short, Iran continues to suffer from psycho-nationalist narcissism.

Yet neither the aggressive realpolitik of the shah, nor the utopian, ideologised foreign policy of the Islamic Republic achieved the aim of global recognition. Neither state managed to systematically construct a politics of identity that would be more subtle and more universal/internationalist than the psycho-nationalism of the political elites at the heart of power allowed for. The meaning of Iran has to be imagined and enacted away from exclusively Persian- or (Shia) Islamo-centric notions, not least because the country's history is heavily laden with global narratives and permeated by world culture, which sit uneasily with hysterical calls for nativist 'authenticity'.[32] Even three decades after the revolution of 1979, the Islamic Republic has not been in the position to implement such an effort, because

---

[32] See further Hamid Dabashi, *The World of Persian Literary Humanism*, 2012.

the indigenous salience of the country's invented Iranian and Shia 'identity' could not be escaped decisively. Both have been intrinsic to the idea of the Islamic Republic and were institutionalised accordingly, beginning with Khomeini's theory of the *velayat-e faqih* which was deeply rooted in Shia political thought, to the decision to retain Twelver Shi'ism (*Ja'fari* school) as Iran's official state religion and the requirement of Iranian origin to qualify for the office of Presidency.[33] The new set of norms projected by the Islamic Republic was hence weaker than pre-existing shared knowledge, inhibiting both the domestic Iranian political culture itself and the regional system – both reproduced and represented the country first and foremost as an Iranian/Shia entity. Hojatoleslam Hassan Yusef Eshkevari, a theorist and proponent of 'Islamic Democracy' in Iran, describes the dilemma in following terms:

> *Velayat-e faqih* is a Sh'i concept of rule. The Sunnis outside of Iran, many of whom doubt that Shi'is are Muslims at all, will therefore never accept this principle. The suspicion with which Sunnis regard the pan-Islamic project of Iran's current government is being fuelled by that very same government, which made Shi'ism the religion of state and reserved all leading governmental positions for Shi'is, all in clear and incontrovertible contradiction to the message of the Islamic Revolution. If the government does not work toward Islamic unity within Iran, how could it do so beyond the country's borders?[34]

The discrepancy between self-perception as a representative pan-Islamic actor and the inherent Iranian/Shia identity of the movement has denied the Islamic Republic the sought after role as the avantgarde of an Islamic movement. Employing theoretical terminology we

---

[33] See Articles 12 and 115 of the Iranian Constitution, respectively.
[34] Quoted in Wilfried Buchta, 'The Failed Pan-Islamic Program of the Islamic Republic: Views of the Liberal Reformers of the Religious "Semi-Opposition"', in Nikki R. Keddie and Rudi Matthee, *Iran and the Surrounding World: Interactions in Culture and Cultural Politics*, Seattle, WA: University of Washington Press, 2002, p. 293.

may observe that the Iranian role remained a subjective self-understanding of the revolutionary state and did not turn into an objective, collectively constituted position or an accepted *role identity* of international structure.[35] The inhibiting norms and institutions of the international system have neither accommodated the idea of a transnational Islamic Republic nor identified Iran as the vanguard of Islamic revivalism. The orbit of Iranian activity abroad has remained confined to primarily Shia circles with established links to the clerical elite in Iran. It is in this way that until today, Iran's imagination of global grandeur has superseded the reality of the country's international power and influence.

---

[35] See further Adib-Moghaddam, *The International Politics of the Persian Gulf*.

3 Geographic Dislocations: Iran Is in India

I have argued that in the course of building a modern nation-state, a project that was given impetus by the Safavid dynasty in the sixteenth century, the political classes governing Iran have developed a psycho-nationalist discourse and a corresponding historical imagination that casts tall shadows on the international affairs of the country. In many ways, psycho-nationalism in Iran indoctrinated a political class to manoeuvre between sudden bouts of hegemonic foreign policies and trying to ensure the mere survival of the state. In both cases and throughout Iran's contemporary history, the elites governing the country never really understood how to take advantage of the multicultural and multi-ethnic composition of the country. They have been quite literally at war with history in order to invent, produce and prove a very particular, rather divisive and retroactive national identity for Iranians. There was no effort to increase the geography of the meaning of Iran which would have required acknowledging a wider historical space for the country.

In this chapter, I will show how at different periods in history the idea of Iran was produced in India, in order to demonstrate that the meaning of Iran transcends geography, even if psycho-nationalism is a strong border-creating device. The construction of any nation radiates beyond the confines of the nation-state and its psycho-nationalist narrators. India is a good place to start my critique of psycho-nationalism and to ease ourselves into the second part of the book which weaves in forms of 'psycho-therapeutic' resistance. Of course, the confines of this book do not allow me to present an exhaustive history of Indo-Iranian relations, and this would not be conducive to my emphasis on psycho-nationalism. Nonetheless, it is possible to sketch some central nodal points holding the Indo-Iranian narrative together in order to show how ideas about nationhood can be dislocated from their usual habitat.[1] To that end, this chapter begins by drawing the contours of what I call an 'Indo-Iranian dialectic' through a survey of cultural exchanges and their impact on religion, literature and politics. This Indo-Iranian dialectic can be conceptualised as a historical imaginary that impinges on the mutual perception of both countries. In many ways India and Iran are embedded within each other. There is then, a stock of shared memory that continuously dislocates the meaning of Iran from its formalised geographic boundaries. The chapter intends to sketch the signposts of that cognitive landscape. Similar chapters could be written about the making of Iran in Turkey, Iraq, Central Asia or Greece.

BURDENS AND OPPORTUNITIES OF HISTORY

The historical interaction of Iran with India is not limited to but was accelerated by the emergence of two Asian empires in the sixteenth century. As discussed in the previous chapters, in Persia, the Safavid dynasty cultivated Shi'ism as the national ideology of the country and constructed the ideational and geopolitical contours out of which the idea of contemporary Iran emerged. This notion of Iran is imbued with a sense of grandeur and entitlement which has lent itself to imperial and hegemonic attitudes towards other nations, especially in Iran's immediate neighbourhood.[2] During the same historical period, in the sixteenth century, the Mughal dynasty established itself in North India. However, this period is not central to understanding contemporary perceptions of India in Iran that arise out of the geopolitical competition between the two emerging Asian empires. Rather, the interaction between Mughal India and Safavid Persia entrenched a

---

[1] Of course there is no suggestion here that there exists an image of India that permeates the mindset of every single Iranian. As we will see, Iranian images of India have fluctuated throughout the centuries. I maintain at the same time that India has a very salient and privileged place in the social construction of national memories in Iran.

[2] See further Arshin Adib-Moghaddam, 'Global Grandeur and the Idea of Iran', in Henner Fuertig (ed.), *Regional Power in the Middle East*, London: Palgrave, 2014, pp. 43–58.

vivid, pre-existing dialectic signposted by rich cultural memories that have impinged on Iran's perception of India and vice versa. Recurrent themes evolve around the following historical signposts: the introduction of Persian as the official language of the Mughal court by the emperor Akbar (1556–1605); his order to teach the Quran in Persian at the proliferating Indian madrasas; the emigration to India by scores of Persian poets, artisans, clergymen, nobility and traders; the great mystical poet Bidel (1644–1721), who emigrated to Delhi and adopted the classical *ghazal* style of poets such as Hafiz and Rumi; Nur Jahan, daughter of a Persian aristocratic family and the queen of emperor Jahangir; architectural manifestations that hybridised the Indo-Iranian interaction further such as the Tomb of Homayun designed by Mir Sayyed Ali and the Taj Mahal with its inscriptions of Persian poetry and its Persian-style gardens; the classic pioneering description of Hinduism by the medieval polymath Abu Raihan Biruni (973–1048), widely considered to be one of the first works in 'Indology';[3] and the intense intermingling of religions, in particular the emigration of persecuted Zoroastrians (Parsis) to India over the centuries.[4] On the one side, this ancient, intimate interaction led to 'perhaps seven times more readers of Persian in the sub-continent than in Iran at the height of the Mughal empire, creating a far-flung network of consumers for travel accounts, chronicles, translations from the Sanskrit, how-to manuals and poetry'.[5] On the other side, 'many of the literary and historical texts edited and published in India achieved canonical status in neighbouring Iran'.[6] Therefore one could say that Iran, during that period, was made in India.

---

[3] Francis Robinson, *Islam in South Asia: Oxford Bibliographies Online Research Guide*, Oxford: Oxford University Press, 2010, p. 10.

[4] See further Mohamad Tavakoli-Targhi, 'Early Persianate Modernity', in Sheldon Pollock (ed.), *Forms of Knowledge in Early Modern Asia: Explorations in the Intellectual History of India and Tibet, 1500–1800*, Durham: Duke University Press, 2011, p. 274.

[5] Juan R. I. Cole, 'Iranian Culture and South Asia, 1500–1900', in Nikki R. Keddie and Rudi Matthee (eds.), *Iran and the Surrounding World: Interactions in Culture and Cultural Politics*, Seattle: University of Washington Press, 2002, p. 31.

[6] Tavakoli-Targhi, 'Early Persianate Modernity', p. 264.

Yet as we will see, the slow demise of this Persophone sphere in the subcontinent after the colonisation of India by the British continues to figure prominently in psycho-nationalist notions of Iran's relations with India (and Pakistan), even after the Islamic revolution of 1979 which was meant to subdue traditional Persianism, at least in the political imagination of Ayatollah Khomeini. Yet as one critic rightly observes: 'The convention of history with borders has created many *homeless texts* that have fallen victim to the fissure of Indian and Iranian nationalism.'[7] Probably the best known, and at the same time one of the most chauvinistic tracts about India which figured prominently in the accounts of Iranian psycho-nationalists was authored by Mohammad Ali Hazin (Shaikh Mohammad Ali Lāhiji, 1692–1766), an aristocrat who fled to Delhi during the reign of Nadir Shah:

> The reason wherefore the Kings of Persia would not retain the government of Hindostan [literally 'province of India' in Persian] in their own hands is manifest to every clear-sighted person. No man, who has a residence and place of abode such as the provinces of Persia afford, which in their nature are the best adjusted and most noble, and to all outward appearance are the most beautiful and perfect habitation in the known world, will ever be able of his own choice to reside in Hindostan. Every person's nature is so formed, that without necessity he will never consent to a long abode in this country; and this feeling is common to the King, the peasant and the soldier. Indeed this is the situation of every man, who with sound senses has been brought up in other air and water, especially if in the empire of Persia or Turkey, unless it be of him who inconsiderately and ignorantly comes into this country, and finds no possibility of returning.[8]

---

[7] Ibid., p. 264, emphasis in original.
[8] Muhammed Ali Hazin, *The Life of Sheikh Mohammed Ali Hazin*, trans. F.C. Belfour, London: Oriental Translation Fund, 1830, p. 279.

In another typical reference point for Iranian psycho-nationalists, Hazin refers to the *Garshapnameh* (The epic of Gershap) authored by Abu Mansour Ali ibn Ahmad Tusi (d. 1072), whom he introduces as the 'master of Ferdowsi'. Ferdowsi wrote the legendary tales of the shahnameh (book of kings) which has been hailed as a marker of Persian identity (in opposition to the Arabs) by luminaries of modern Iranian psycho-nationalism such as Taqizadeh, Kermani and Akhundzadeh, as I have argued in Chapter 1. Hazin adapts a section of Tusi's *Garshapnameh* in which the legendary figure of Zahhak gives the following order to Garshap, the commander of his troops:

> He thus gave instructions to Garshap:
> In India bid adieu to sleep.
> Spare not the blood of the soldiers,
> But continually put in action the flaming sword.
> With speed make an end of your important business,
> And strike on them as a wolf on a flock of sheep.
> Stay not the year out in that country.
> Lest the army step aside from fame and valour.
> Should four seasons pass over you there,
> You would no longer find a trace of manlihood or bravery.[9]

Of course, I am not quoting from these sections in order to suggest that there is an unchanging chauvinistic attitude inherent in Iranian imaginations about India. As Mana Kia has rightly argued in her wide-ranging study of the writings of Hazin, thinking Hazin's view of Hindustan emblematic of Iranian 'proto-nationalism . . . obfuscates overlapping ideas of exile, home and the importance of specific historical events to the changing shape of Persianate culture, which for the Iranians of the first half of the eighteenth century was the fall of the Safavid state'.[10] One could take this statement one step further

---

[9] Ibid., p. 281.
[10] Mana Kia, 'Accounting for Difference: A Comparative Look at the Autobiographical Travel Narratives of Hazin Lahiji and Abd-al-Karim Kashmiri', *Journal of Persianate Studies*, Vol. 2 (2009), p. 212.

and argue that even the most aggressive tracts about another community always also reify the presence of that presumed 'other' as a significant part of the 'self'.[11] From that perspective India has been an important interlocutor of Iranian history even when it was deemed a competitor for imperial domination in Asia or 'culturally depleted' as in the writings of Hazin.

A potent, untapped Indo-Iranian space is laid open here, which has been minimised, however, by the cloistered histories written by psycho-nationalist historians in both India and Iran. The controversy over the so-called *Sabke-Hendi* (Indian style) and especially the poetry of Bidel serves as a good example in that regard. Indian and Iranian commentators with a psycho-nationalist conviction have been engaged in a relentless feud about the merits of the Indo-Persian poetry cultivated by the Mughal court. In his examination of Persian literary humanism, Hamid Dabashi correctly observes that 'obvious and evident in this very assessment is the ahistorical *nationalisation* of Persian literary heritage and the entirely flawed division suggested between "mainline Iranian poetry" and Indian style poetry'. He goes on to make an important link between the colonial period and such (psycho)nationalised histories of the meaning of Iran and Persia, deeming them a 'deeply defective categorisation of Persian poetic traditions along postcolonial national boundaries that did not exist, nor did they decide literary and poetic tastes, at the time of the Mughal Empire'.[12]

There are at least three historical factors that explain why the Indo-Iranian dialectic interrupted modernity so dramatically, in particular in the period between the late eighteenth and early twentieth century. First, the invasion of India by the Afshar monarch Nadir Shah (d. 1747) when he conquered Kandahar and entered Delhi in 1738,

---

[11] I have theorised this notion in Adib-Moghaddam, *On the Arab Revolts and the Iranian Revolution: Power and Resistance Today*, New York: Bloomsbury, 2013, in particular interregnum 6 and 7.
[12] Hamid Dabashi, *The World of Persian Literary Humanism*, Cambridge: Harvard University Press, 2012, p. 208.

returning to Iran, it is said, with the legendary peacock throne and the *koohi-noor* diamond (which subsequently ended up in the crown of Queen Victoria and eventually Queen Elizabeth II). The invasion put an end to centuries of complimentary political and cultural relations which were only occasionally disturbed by geopolitical competition in Central and South Asia.

The impact of western imperialism was equally devastating. The British efforts to minimise the Asian heritage of India led to a concerted campaign to replace Persian as a language of administration including in the higher law courts. This goal was codified in the English Education Act of 1835 which was emblematic of what Edward Said aptly criticised as 'Orientalism'.[13] In an infamous 'minute on Indian education', the chief sponsor of the Act, the liberal English politician Thomas Babington Macaulay, justified the new policy in typical Orientalist parlance as a responsibility to stop teaching 'languages, by which, by universal confession, there are no books on any subject which deserve to be compared to our own'.[14] In his defence of the Act, Macaulay pointed out that he had contact with 'men distinguished by their proficiency in the Eastern tongues'.[15] But these contacts were a disappointment because he could not find 'any among them who could deny that a single shelf of a good European library was worth the whole native literature of India and Arabic'.[16] Therefore it was necessary to cultivate 'a class of persons, Indian in blood and colour, but English in tastes, in opinions, in morals, and in intellect'. To that class England should bestow the responsibility to 'refine the vernacular dialectics of the country, to enrich those

---

[13] See further Edward Said, *Orientalism*, London: Penguin, 1995. Recent reflections on the debate can be found in Ian Richard Netton (ed.), *Orientalism Revisited: Art, Land and Voyage*, London: Routledge, 2013.

[14] 'Minute Recorded in the General Department by Thomas Babington Macaulay, law member of the governor-general's council, dated 2 February 1835', in Lynn Zastoupil and Martin Moir (eds.), *The Great Indian Education Debate: Documents Relating to the Orientalist-Anglicist Controversy, 1781–1843*, London: Routledge, 2013, p. 166.

[15] Ibid., p. 165.

[16] Ibid.

dialects with terms of science borrowed from the Western nomenclature, and to render them by degrees fit vehicles for conveying knowledge to the great mass of the population'.[17]

A third factor that challenged the Indo-Iranian dialectic can be ascribed to the psycho-nationalisation of historical memory and the narrow spatialisation of the meaning of Iran around stringent ethnocentric and linguistic norms, especially in the mid-nineteenth and early twentieth century. The late Qajar kings already experimented with a notion of Iranian superiority which was increasingly coded in ethnocentric language. 'If travellers show justice [in evaluating] the correct temperament, customs and faiths of Iranians', Mumtahin al-Dawlah, a prominent Qajar statesman pointed out emblematically for his period, 'they would see the superiority that nature has conferred upon the land, and people of Iran'.[18] Such attitudes proclaiming inherent Iranian superiority permeated the writings of many scholars and statesman during the Qajar period. And as I have repeatedly pointed out: influential Iranian psycho-nationalists such as Akhundzadeh, Kermani and Taqizadeh inscribed into the narrative of Iran an insidiously hegemonic attitude towards neighbouring countries that was inimical to Persia's multicultural, multiethnic composition. The Pahlavis followed this trend even more stringently and emphasised the skewed notion that Iranians were first and foremost 'Aryan'. As such, the mythology of the Pahlavis favoured Iran's pre-Islamic heritage and rationalised proclivity to the 'west' as the ideal civilisational model to be adopted in Iran and beyond. Hence, Asia lost much of its cultural and political appeal.

These hermetic inventions of the meaning of Iran narrowed the geo-cultural boundaries of the country and minimised them to a perverted Persian essence divorced from its cosmopolitan heritage. Hence, Iranians were increasingly seen as racially superior to other

---

[17] Ibid., p. 171.
[18] Quoted in Firoozeh Kashani-Sabet, *Frontier Fictions: Shaping the Iranian Nation 1804–1946*, Princeton: Princeton University Press, 1999, p. 47.

peoples of the world and quite distinct in their culture and traditions. With the emergence of such ethnocentric tropes in Iranian psycho-nationalist discourse, India neither was considered a cultural partner, nor could be a political one. Under the influence of Orientalist notions emphasising the inherent superiority of the western world, Iranian psycho-nationalists increasingly discarded Persia's Indian and eastern heritage. It should not come as a surprise then that it was during this period that the Indian poetic style that I previously mentioned was deemed by literary historians such as Muhammad Taqi Bahar (1886–1951) to be inferior to 'mainstream' Persian poetry.[19] Galvanised by the ethnocentric psycho-nationalism espoused by the first Pahlavi monarch, Reza Shah (1878–1944), Iranian elites reverted to racialised notions of Iranian-ness that were devoid of multicultural breadth. Therefore, apart from loose references to a presumably common 'Aryan' ancestry ascribed to Iranians and Indians alike by Kermani and Taqizadeh, an enduring myth reinterpreted from the writings of European Orientalists such as Gobineau (1816–82), Renan (1823–92) and Edward B. Browne (1862–1926), India was almost obliterated as a topic in Iran in the early to mid-twentieth century, despite the rich Indo-Persian field that the interaction between Safavid Iran and Moghul India had engendered.

GEOPOLITICAL REDISCOVERIES

After the Second World War, the rupture in the Indo-Iranian dialectic outlined above was compounded by strategic estrangement due to the pro-American foreign policy adopted by Mohammad Reza Shah (1919–80), which was at odds with India's involvement with the Non-Alignment Movement and the tilt towards the Soviet Union during the Cold War. Iran entered into alignment with the west via CENTO (Central Treaty Organisation) which brought together the United Kingdom, Iraq, Turkey and indeed Pakistan much to the ire of Indian Prime Minister Nehru who strongly denounced the pact. Moreover,

---

[19] Hamid Dabashi, *Persian Literary Humanism*, p. 209.

Iran was the first country to officially recognise Pakistan in 1947. In 1948, diplomatic relations were established and the shah became the first foreign head of state to visit the country two years later. In contrast, Iran and India only established formal diplomatic relations in 1950. CENTO obliged the shah to support Pakistan during the Indo-Pakistani conflict in 1965 and the subsequent war in 1971 which complicated relations with India even further. However, the shah continued to have cordial relations with India throughout the 1960s and 1970s, especially relating to economic interests. At the same time, the two countries could never really transmute relations into a strategic partnership due to their clashing alliance patterns.

Ironically, while the postcolonial period destroyed much of the Indo-Persian dialectic, it also created a new field into which some of the rather more contemporary Iranian attitudes towards India have been pasted. In the period after the Second World War, Iranian revolutionaries, both secular and with Islamist persuasion, increasingly looked at the independence struggle in the subcontinent as a model to rid Iran from the Pahlavi monarchy and its westernising policies. As a consequence, India appeared in the historical imagination of major Iranian thinkers and politicians as a model for 'anti-imperial' resistance. For Iran's first democratically elected Prime Minister, Mohammad Mossadegh, for instance, Gandhi 'was a rare human being who, with a miraculous technique, brought India up to the heights on which she stands today'.[20] Indicative of his democratic convictions, Mossadegh also praised Gandhi for his attempts to subdue religious difference and sectarianism on the subcontinent, labelling him a 'great supporter of Indian Muslims . . . Ghandhiji not only stabilised the greatness of his country in his own life-time', Mossadegh added, 'but also left behind men like Jawaharlal Nehru who is a finished product of the Gandhi school'.[21] Inspired by the

[20] 'Mossadegh Hails Mahatma Gandhi', *The Hindu*, 1 February 1952. Available at www.hindu.com/2002/02/01/stories/2002020103250600.htm (accessed 2 December 2013).
[21] Ibid.

non-violent resistance strategies of Gandhi and the staunch anti-imperialism of Nehru,[22] Mossadegh went on to nationalise the Anglo-Iranian-Oil Company in 1951.[23] Two years later he was deposed by an MI6/CIA engineered coup d'état which reinstated the authoritarian monarchy of the shah, Mohammad Reza Pahlavi. Yet despite his short spell in power, Mossadegh continues to cast tall shadows on the historical imagination of Iran's intelligentsia – references to Gandhi and Nehru are abundant in that regard.[24]

While Iran's anti-colonial nationalists (not the psycho-nationalists) highlighted the legacy of Nehru and Gandhi along the themes of religious tolerance and national independence, the emerging Islamic intellectuals claimed Gandhi and Muhammad Iqbal (Lahori) for their revolutionary struggle. Rather, from the perspective of these revolutionaries, Gandhi and Iqbal were heroes of national independence. The fact that Iqbal was appropriated by Pakistan and ostracised from the official historical memory of India was secondary to such inventions. Iqbal was celebrated because of his writings in Persian and the renewal of Islam that he advocated, and he was represented as an Indo-Muslim nodal point in the anti-colonial struggles on the subcontinent. While postcolonial India and Gandhi were cast as great examples for the viability of such resistance, Iqbal became a focal point for the success of Islamic politics.[25] Therefore, in the narratives of the most influential Islamic revolutionaries in Iran, he appears as a heroic defendant of national independence *and* Islamic resurgence.

---

[22] Prithvi Ram Mudiam, *India and the Middle East*, London: I.B. Tauris, 1994, p. 70.

[23] See further Ervand Abrahamian, *The Coup 1953, the CIA and the Roots of Modern US-Iranian Relations*, New York: New Press, 2013.

[24] See among others Hamid Dabashi, 'Mossadegh and the Legacy of Non Aligned Movement' *Al-Jazeera*, 26 August 2012. Available at www.aljazeera.com/indepth/opinion/2012/08/201282681749809950.html (accessed 18 January 2014); Ramin Jahanbegloo, *The Gandhian Moment*, Cambridge, MA: Harvard University Press, 2013 and Behzad Yaghmaian, *Social Change in Iran: An Eyewitness Account of Dissent, Defiance, and New Movements for Rights*, New York: State University of New York Press, 2002, p. 239.

[25] The Islamist revolutionaries took particular inspiration from the writings and poetry of Iqbal, while Iran's liberal factions leaned towards the non-violent methods of Gandhi. After the revolution, the city council of Tehran even went so far as to name two major streets in the Iranian capital after Gandhi and Iqbal, respectively.

As such, Ali Shariati described him as the forerunner of an Islamic renaissance.[26] Moreover, the current Supreme Leader of Iran, Ali Khamenei, without the references to religious pluralism and democracy that Shariati included in his writings, authored a book titled *The Role of Muslims in the Independence Struggle of India* in which Iqbal figures prominently. In a seminar dedicated to Iqbal held in Tehran in 1986, Khamenei expressed his admiration for him in vivid terms:

> The particular conditions in our country, especially the political domination of the colonialist powers during the last years of Iqbal's life in his favourite country, Iran, never allowed Iqbal to visit this country . . . Today the Islamic Republic (i.e. the embodiment of Iqbal's dream) has been established here, Iqbal . . . had he been alive today, he could have seen a nation standing on its feet, infused with the rich Islamic spirit and drawing upon the inexhaustible reservoirs of Islamic heritage, a nation which has become self-sufficient and has discarded all the glittering Western ornaments and is marching ahead courageously, determining its own targets and moving to attain them, advancing with the frenzy of a lover, and has not imprisoned itself within the walls of nationalism and racialism . . . Our people have translated into action his doctrine of the selfhood. They have invigorated it and have brought it into action in the world of actuality . . . Today we are perfectly aware of being on our feet. We are proud of our culture and our cultural heritage, and are confident that we can develop it further on the basis of our ideology and thought. As Iqbal has said repeatedly, we can learn the modern science and philosophy from the West, but the ardour and zest for life can never be borrowed from others:
>
> *Wisdom we have learnt from the teachings of the Western thinkers.*

---

[26] Iqbal Singh Sevea, *The Political Philosophy of Muhammad Iqbal: Islam and Nationalism in Late Colonial India*, Cambridge: Cambridge University Press, 2012, p. 201. See also Ali Shariati and Sayyid Ali Khamene'i, *Manifestation of the Islamic Spirit*, trans. Mahliqa Qara'i and Laleh Bakhtiar, Markham, Ontario: Open Press, 1991.

> *Ardour for life we have acquired in the company of men of insight.*

> It means that the Western society and culture is wanting in ardour and fervour, and Iqbal was quicker than any other person in perceiving this phenomenon. He could anticipate the dangers inherent in the Western civilisation and its materialistic culture, and warned the people in advance that it was devoid of the spiritual elements essential for human welfare. Fortunately, today the consciousness of selfhood and Islamic identity is abounding in our country among the people. Our policy based on the principle of 'Neither the East nor the West' is in conformity with what Iqbal advised and wished to be pursued. Our policy of self-reliance is identical with Iqbal's views.[27]

The themes of anti-colonialism, eastern spirituality (versus western materialism), Irano-centric psycho-nationalism and (Islamist) identity construction that were so central to the Khomeinist factions of the Iranian revolution are apparent here. Khamenei is clearly positioning Iran at the centre of his narrative, almost appropriating Iqbal himself as an Iranian. In a rather patronising passage towards the end of his speech he even went so far as to demand the Pakistani and Indian delegates present at the conference to spearhead efforts to reintroduce Persian as a major language in the subcontinent:

> This work has been done in Pakistan to some extent, but the people of Pakistan cannot be fully benefited from those ideas as today the Persian language is not in currency there as in the past. I wish this gap also to be filled. It is further hoped that our Pakistani brothers present in this meeting as well as the writers

---

[27] Sayyid Ali Khamene'i, *Iqbal: The Poet Philosopher of Islamic Resurgence*. Speech delivered at the opening session of the First International Conference on Iqbal, held at Tehran, 10–12 March 1986, on the occasion of the 108th birth anniversary of the poet of the Subcontinent. Translated by Mahliqa Qara'i. Available at http://islam-pure.de/imam/books/iqbal.htm (accessed 12 November 2013).

of the Indian subcontinent realise their responsibility and rise to the occasion to resist the vicious policies of the past governments regarding the Persian language, which possesses great treasures of Islamic culture and in which the major part of Islamic culture is preserved. They should give currency to this language in the Subcontinent where there are great numbers of Muslims; especially in Pakistan this work needs to be done with a sense of urgency.[28]

The tensions in these sections are reflective of the real political dilemma that the Iranian revolution created for itself and others in international affairs. On the one side, Asia had to become central to Iran's foreign policy. Even before the revolution, Khomeini put particular emphasis on the importance of such an 'eastern' orientation as a means to foil what he described as a divide and rule strategy of the west; a 'conspiracy' by imperialists to subjugate the 'oppressed' people of the world in general and the 'east' in particular:

> The imperialist governments, those governments that seek to plunder the wealth of Muslims, deceive the Islamic countries, the heads of Islamic countries, through different means and numerous tricks . . . Disturbances are created between Hindus and Muslims, between the Indian sects, resulting in disputes which attract a lot of attention. They use these disputes to devour the East.[29]

In accordance with the shift away from the west, Iran opted out of CENTO and became a member of – and assumed a proactive role in – the Non-Alignment Movement. The importance of India to this reorientation was acknowledged from the outset. In 1981, the current Supreme Leader of Iran, Khamenei, visited India as a member of the Revolutionary Council and met with Prime Minister Indira Gandhi

---

[28] Ibid.

[29] 'The Imam's speech to religious students, clerics, merchants of the bazaar and other resident in Qum', Az'am Mosque, Qum, 9 September 1964. Available at www.imam-khomeini.com/web1/english/showitem.aspx?pid=-1&cid=1203 (accessed 21 December 2013).

and the then External Affairs Minister Narasimha Rao in order to forge closer relations between the two countries.[30] Undoubtedly, the interest in India, and the history of anti-colonial struggles in the subcontinent more generally, were not spurned merely by strategic calculations. There was also a good deal of cultural curiosity involved. Yet while the discourse of anti-imperialism resonated with India's political elites, the Islamo-centric focus of the new rulers and shrill proclamations about changing the world order triggered alarm bells in Delhi. Iran after the revolution was still beset with psycho-nationalist hubris, this time imbued with Islamist symbols and imagery which remained distinctly Irano-centric. As a consequence, the immediate attempts of Iran to forge closer ties with India around the themes of 'non-alignment' and 'anti-imperialism' after the revolution of 1979 were largely fruitless. India, while keen to continue to secure oil supplies from Tehran, did not react to Iranian overtures to support the country after it was invaded by Saddam Hussein's Iraq in 1980. As the leader of the Non-Aligned Movement at that time, Indira Gandhi insisted on keeping a neutral and equidistant stance that prioritised access to both oil markets. Thus, India and Iran remained estranged ideational bedfellows.

The end of the Iran–Iraq war in 1988 and the death of Ayatollah Khomeini one year later changed the foreign policies of Iran.[31] Under the leadership of Khamenei as the new Supreme Guide of the Islamic Republic, and in tandem with the Presidency of Ali-Akbar Hashemi Rafsanjani between 1990 and 97, Iran pursued a rather more pragmatic path in international affairs. Rafsanjani focused on rebuilding the country's tattered diplomatic relations, with a particular emphasis on Iran's immediate neighbourhood. As a result of this shift away from

---

[30] Khamenei mentioned this at a recent meeting with Manmohan Singh. He also invoked the legacy of both Nehru and Gandhi. See 'Iran's Khamenei remembers Gandhi-Nehru in his meeting with Manmohan Singh', *New Delhi Television*, 30 August 2012. Available at www.ndtv.com/article/india/iran-s-khamenei-remembers-gandhi-nehru-in-his-meeting-with-manmohan-singh-260761 (accessed 11 December 2013).

[31] See further Arshin Adib-Moghaddam, *The International Politics of the Persian Gulf*.

the radical policies of the first decade after the revolution, relations between Iran and India quickly improved: Prime Minister Narasimha Rao visited Iran in 1993 and Rafsanjani reciprocated in 1995. Cultural interactions picked up as well and were accelerated by the visit of the former President of Iran, Mohammad Khatami, in 1994 as the then Head of the Iranian National Library.[32] Crucially, Iran also initiated a subtle shift away from supporting Pakistan on the issue of Kashmir. Before the revolution and under the radical leadership of Ayatollah Khomeini, Iran was supportive of the Pakistani position. In the first decade after the revolution of 1979, movements such as the *Jamaate Islami of Jammu and Kashmir* actively sought and received the pan-Islamic support of the Iranian revolutionaries.[33] After the death of Khomeini, however, Iran initiated a gradual shift away from that policy. Despite rhetorical references to the freedom-fighting people of Kashmir, successive Iranian governments tip-toed around the issue and emphasised that the solution of the crisis would be dependent on rapprochement between India and Pakistan, reducing the matter, in effect, to the bilateral relations of the two countries.[34]

While it is true to argue that with the demise of the Soviet Union as a strategic partner of India and the onset of the 'unipolar moment' in world politics characterised by the dominance of the United States immediately after the end of the Cold War in the early 1990s, India veered towards Washington, it is equally accurate that the country's leaders were careful not to jeopardise relations with Iran whose political elites remained trapped in the anti-American discourse of the first decade of the revolution. India pursued a delicate balancing act and reaped the fruits of better relations with both Iran and the United States in the 1990s. The newly found partnership with

---

[32] For a comprehensive of the Khatami presidency in Iran see Ghoncheh Tazmini, *Khatami's Iran: The Islamic Republic and the Turbulent Path to Reform*, London: I.B Tauris, 2009.
[33] Yoginder S. Sikand, 'The Jama'at-i-Islami of Jammu and Kashmir', in Paul R. Brass and Achin Vanaik (eds.), *Competing Nationalisms in South Asia: Essays for Asghar Ali Engineer*, London: Sangam Books Ltd., pp. 272–273.
[34] Aparna Pande, *Explaining Pakistan's Foreign Policy: Escaping India*, London: Routledge, 2011, p. 141.

Iran peaked with a visit to Delhi by the former President Mohammad Khatami, a reformist cleric whose dialogue among civilisations theme was adopted by the United Nations as the political motto for the year 2001. A year earlier India had agreed to build a North-South Corridor expanding the Iranian port of Chahbahar with access to the Indian Ocean linking it to the Afghan city Zaranj and to the newly independent states of Central Asia (and from there to Russia).

Furthermore, Khatami visited India in 2003 as the chief guest on the occasion of India's republican day celebrations, a distinct honour only granted to the closest allies of the country. While in Delhi, Khatami finalised negotiations that started with the 'Tehran Declaration' in 2001 between him and Prime Minister Vajpayee who had visited Iran with a high-ranking delegation which included senior military and security personnel. As a result, both leaders signed the 'New Delhi Declaration' in January 2003 which formalised the close relations between the two countries along several cultural, economic and political themes.[35] First, India and Iran committed themselves to furthering a 'strategic dialogue' institutionalised in meetings of the 'Joint Commission [and] interaction between the Security Councils of the two countries, discussions on energy and security . . . supplies, exploration, investment, exchange of technical expertise, and other interaction at government and private sector levels'. The Declaration uses terms such as 'strategic convergence', 'complementarity of interests' and 'strategic and long-term orientation to the bilateral relationship' to emphasise the importance of the document. It also refers to a 'common cultural heritage rooted in history of the two countries' which is indicative of the cultural dialectic that I attempted to outline in the first part of this chapter.[36] The point is that once psycho-nationalist tropes were subdued in Iran's foreign policy, the diplomatic space and connectibility of the country increased.

---

[35] For the declaration see 'The Republic of India and the Islamic Republic of Iran: The "New Delhi" declaration'. Available at www.satp.org/satporgtp/countries/india/document/papers/iran_delhidecl.htm (accessed 26 January 2014).

[36] Ibid.

As a consequence, the strategic partnership envisaged did not stop short of cooperation in the sensitive security sector. The geopolitical context was important in that regard: in the 1990s, India and Iran worked in tandem (with Russia) in order to bolster the Northern Alliance in Afghanistan which was fighting a relentless civil war against the Taliban. From the Indian perspective, the fact that the Taliban was supported by Pakistan gave this strategic theatre particular significance. Iran closely liaised with India about Afghanistan but at the same time attempted to bring Pakistan into the fold with the so-called 'peace pipeline' which would carry Iranian gas to both Pakistan and India.[37] Afghanistan, then, was a central factor in the burgeoning Indo-Iranian security relations at that time. As a result, two months after the New Delhi Declaration, warships from India and Iran conducted a joint naval exercise, consultations between security and intelligence personnel was routinised, the exchange of military equipment accelerated and India was increasingly involved in training segments of the Iranian army.[38]

The New Delhi Declaration must be seen as the apotheosis of Indo-Iranian relations in the post-independence period. It is true,

---

[37] India never fully committed to the project. The Iranian part of the pipeline leading to Pakistan has been finished and there has been recent movement to finalise the project despite the cancellation of an Iranian loan to finance the construction of the pipeline in Pakistan. See 'Iran cancels Pakistan gas pipeline loan', *Bloomberg News*, 14 December 2013. Available at www.businessweek.com/ap/2013-12-14/iran-cancels-pakistan-gas-pipeline-loan (accessed 1 January 2014). See also Abbas Maleki, 'Iran-Pakistan-India Pipeline: Is It a Peace Pipeline?', *MIT Center for International Studies Audit of the Conventional Wisdom*, Vol. 7, No. 16, September 2007. Available at http://web.mit.edu/cis/pdf/Audit_09_07_Maleki.pdf (accessed 12 January 2014).

[38] See Robert M. Hathaway, 'The "Strategic" Partnership between India and Iran', *Asia Program Special Report*, No. 120, April 2004, p. 1. Available at www.wilsoncenter.org/sites/default/files/asia_rpt_120rev_0.pdf (accessed 14 January 2014). There have been news reports that indicate that Iran even offered to open Iranian military facilities to the Indian army in the case of a conflict with Pakistan while in return India offered to: facilitate warship repair facilities at Iran's aforementioned Chahbahar port at the Indian Ocean; send Indian army engineers to Iranian military bases to maintain and upgrade Iran's fleet of Russian-made MIG 29 fighters, T-72 tanks, infantry fighting vehicles and tower artillery guns; aid Iran's space programme and sell Konkurs anti-tank guided weapons and spare parts to Iran. See Vivek Raghuvanshi, 'India-Iran sign strategic record'. *DefenseNews.com*, 23 January 2003.

as I indicated above, that with the onset of the so-called unipolar moment after the demise of the Soviet Union, the political elites in India seemed to have realised that closer relations with the United States were inevitable in order to sustain India's economic growth and that the United States was needed to balance against the rise of China as a pan-Asian powerhouse with global aspirations. This opening to the United States manifested itself in a robust US-Indian strategic dialogue with increasing security entanglements. In addition, India moved to establish full diplomatic relations with Israel in 1992, a notable change in policy given that India was among the states that voted against the establishment of Israel in the UN vote of 1948.[39] Certainly, this proclivity towards the United States eclipsed Indo-Iranian relations (in a less dramatic manner compared with the impact of colonial Britain and psycho-nationalist agitation outlined above). Concurrently, it should be noted that the visit of Khatami on India's republican day came amidst heightened tensions between Washington and Tehran. The Bush administration had labelled Iran a member of the infamous 'axis of evil' (together with North Korea and Iraq) that needed to be combated. Washington was buzzing with the discourse of war and foreign invasions. Yet India and Iran dared to forge a strategic partnership despite the divisive zeitgeist of the 'War on Terror'.

The American factor was particularly pronounced with regard to the nuclear energy programme of Iran. Both Iran and the United States increasingly lobbied New Delhi to take their side in international forums, forcing Delhi to choose between a rock and a hard place. India is principally opposed to nuclear proliferation. At the same time it does not support the sanctions regime enforced by the United States. Therefore, India tried to balance its votes against Iran in the IAEA with a concerted drive against US sanctions and the threat of war. This is one of the reasons why India supported the Brazil–Turkey–Iran nuclear deal which was aimed at creating a dual track

---

[39] Hathaway, 'The "Strategic" Partnership between India and Iran', p. 4.

to the confrontation with the west. It also explains why to date India remains among the few countries that continues to import oil from Iran despite the stringent, US-led sanctions regime. The danger of escalation came to haunt India on its own territory when in February 2013 bombs went off in front of the Israeli embassy in New Delhi. Hawks in Tel Aviv and Washington were quick to blame Iran despite the lack of conclusive evidence to that end.[40] Ultimately, India managed to smooth out relations between the Ahmadinejad Presidency and the Bush administration in the United States. Currently, India is watching with eager anticipation as to whether or not the Iranian-American détente can continue. India has been quick to signal the incentives to Iran: it has recently committed US $100 million to upgrade facilities at the Chahbahar port if Iran and the United States find a diplomatic solution to the nuclear file and if sanctions are lifted. This strategic move would take full advantage of the Indian-built 220-km road connecting the port with the infrastructure in western Afghanistan and from there to Central Asia and Russia.

THE LIMITS OF GEOGRAPHY

The historical memory binding India and Iran together and the hybrid field into which the Indo-Iranian dialectic has repeatedly unfolded itself has been recurrently referred to by intellectuals and scholars in both countries. This should not be considered mere rhetoric. Contemporary Indo-Iranian relations are deepening in the cultural realm exactly because of an increasing awareness of that common ideational space.[41] Yet at the same time, states are bound to pursue what they perceive to be in their 'national interest' and India and Iran are no exceptions. Psycho-nationalism narrows such perceptions

---

[40] See further Arshin Adib-Moghaddam, 'Iran Seems an Unlikely Culprit for the Attacks on Israeli Diplomats', *The Guardian*, 15 February 2012. Available at www.theguardian.com/commentisfree/2012/feb/15/iran-israeli-diplomats-attacks (accessed 12 December 2012).

[41] Raja Karthikeya, 'India's Iran Calculus', *Foreign Policy*, 24 September 2010. Available at http://mideastafrica.foreignpolicy.com/posts/2010/09/24/indias_iran_calculus (accessed 1 February 2012).

of 'national interest' because psycho-nationalism feeds into a form of nationalist narcissism that is anathema to coherent, consistent and peaceful diplomacy. Whenever Iranian decision-makers subdued their psycho-nationalist discourse, for instance during the reformist Khatami Presidency, the international relations of the country improved. Whenever there was a hysterical call for arms in the name of a cloistered identity, Iran was isolated. The point is that the strategic preferences of any country are informed by inventions of national identity which constitute how the 'national interest' is defined in the first place. Psycho-nationalism tilts this interest to an elite group at the heart of power and deprives others from the spoils of international engagements. In this way, the majority of Iranians have suffered from psycho-nationalism, in terms of both their domestic politics and the international image of the country.

4 Religious Neuroses: Islam and the People

I have already started to show that in the revolutionary process that delivered the Islamic Republic in 1979, something rather novel happened in Iran. For the first time in world history, a state endowed itself with both a republican mandate and a religious, clerically centred sovereignty. The leadership of the supreme jurisprudent (*Velayat-e faqih*), theorised by Khomeini in exile in Najaf in the 1970s, is at the heart of this institutional make-up of the Iranian state. In this chapter, I will disentangle some of the foundations of power that underlie the system of the *Velayat-e faqih* in order to unravel its psycho-nationalist dynamics and nuances. I will show how in the build up to the post-revolutionary state, the nature of power of the *faqih* changed from a religious-theological ideal-type to a pragmatist-realist one. I maintain that both are driven by psycho-nationalist dynamics, as mentioned in the previous chapters. In terms of its hubristic core, the institution of the Supreme Leader is as narcissistic as the title of the shah-in-shah, or king of kings. Both forms of sovereignty are restrictive in terms of their prescriptions for Iran's national identity (and by extension the national interest of the country, as discussed in the previous chapter).

If Ayatollah Khomeini was a revolutionary cleric who brought about sudden and radical change in Iran and beyond, his successor Khamenei appears as a pragmatist 'prefect' of Khomeini's contested political legacy, whose foundations of power are far more sober and formalised than those of the late leader of the Iranian revolution. Both leaders have strengthened and perfected the psycho-nationalist tropes in Iranian politics. After the revolution, repeatedly there was room to negotiate them – as we have seen, the thermidor of Khatami changed some of the dynamics certainly in terms of Iran's international relations. To a lesser extent, the current President Hassan Rouhani has managed to contain some of the nationalist narcissism that I have talked about in the previous chapters, certainly in the international affairs of Iran which made it easier to find a diplomatic solution to the nuclear file and engender cautious détente with the United States. But in the end the *Vali-e faqih* must be analysed as an extension of psycho-nationalist sovereignty and legitimacy in the contemporary history of Iran, with all the baggage that this brings. Therefore, dissecting the major tenets of this institution of the Supreme Leader will put us in a better position to assess the nuances of current trends in Iranian psycho-nationalism.

A (SHORT) GENEALOGY OF THE SUPREME JURISPRUDENT

By all standards, Ayatollah Khomeini was a giant of the twentieth century. The Iranian revolution of 1979, which unfolded so eclectically under his leadership, quite literally shook the world. Like all giants of history, Khomeini left an indelible imprint on the consciousness of his people, a stock of shared memories that is constituted by nostalgia, reverence, utopia and loyalty on the one side and exile, tragedy, hatred and rejection on the other. Comparable to the impact of other revolutionary leaders of the twentieth century – Lenin, Mao, Castro – Khomeini's era seriously affected both the personal life of the people he eventually came to govern and the trajectory of world politics.

By virtue of their gigantic projects, revolutionary leaders claim history in its entirety. Theirs is, by definition, a rebellion against the planetary order that promises to bring about universal, not relative, change. So, too, Khomeini in 1979 was not a reformist; he was not in Iran to compromise with the ancien régime of the shah. He was there to define, once and for all, what he considered to be the ideal political and social order for human beings, which he thought applicable not only to Iran but throughout the globe. As he proclaimed from exile in Neauphle-le-Chateau at the height of the revolutionary fervour in that fateful winter of 1978/9:

> Great People of Iran! The history of Iran, even world history, has never witnessed a movement like yours; it has never experienced a universal uprising like yours, noble people! . . . Our lionhearted women snatch up their infants and go to confront the machine guns and tanks of the regime; where in history has such valiant and heroic behaviour by women been recorded? . . . Fear nothing in your pursuit of these Islamic goals, for no power can halt this great movement. You are in the right; the hand of God Almighty is with you and it is His will that those who have been oppressed should assume leadership and become heirs to their own destiny and resources.[1]

Revolutionaries strive to establish a new order in word and deed and are not satisfied with reforms or token amendments to the state and the socio-economic system in place. To that end, Khomeini targeted history from a radical standpoint. Also always concerned with legacy, memory and method, he was aware that the revolution had to be grandiose and performed as such. 'It is important for the awakening of future generations and the prevention of distortions by partial opponents [*moqrezan*],' he wrote in the preface to a prominent book about him published three years after the revolution, 'that fellow writers correctly analyse the history of this Islamic movement and transcribe the exact dates and motivation behind the demonstrations and revolts of Iran's Muslims in the various provinces'.[2] Here and elsewhere, Khomeini spoke in momentous terms: world history, nobility, God, universality, heroism, Islam, greatness – these are the

---

[1] Ruhollah Khomeini, 'In Commemoration of the Martyrs of Tehran, October 11, 1978', in Hamid Algar (ed., trans.), *Islam and Revolution I: Writings and Declarations of Imam Khomeini*, London: Mizan Press, 1981, pp. 240–1.

[2] Seyyed Hamid Rouhani (Ziarati), *Baresi va tahlil az nehzate Imam Khomeini*, 11th edition, Tehran: Entesharat-e Rahe Imam, 1360 [1982].

ingredients of his psycho-nationalist discourse which was geared towards the revolutionary momentum that Iranians were driving.

The preamble to the constitution of the Islamic Republic of Iran which was adopted by referendum on 24 October 1979 reiterated that message. It describes the revolution as 'unique' in comparison to previous Iranian revolts such as the 'anti-despotic movement for constitutional government' in 1906, and the 'anti-colonialist movement for the nationalisation of petroleum' led by Mohammad Mossadegh between 1951 and 3. 'The Muslim people of Iran' learnt the lessons of history because 'they realised that the basic and specific reason for the failure of those movements was that they were not religious ones'. As opposed to those previous disappointments, 'the nation's conscience has awakened to the leadership of an exalted Authority, His Eminence Ayatollah Imam Khomeini, and has grasped the necessity of following the line of the true religious and Islamic movement'. Followed by a long section on Khomeini's central role in leading the revolution headlined 'The Vanguard of the Movement', it is further stated that Iran's 'militant clergy, which has always been in the front lines of the people's movement, together with writers and committed intellectuals, has gained new strength [lit: impetus] under his leadership'.[3] Quite from the outset then, there was no doubt about the importance of Khomeini to the legitimation of the revolutionary process in Iran. It is this centrality to the revolution, spearheaded by Iranians from all walks of life, that turned him into a personality and topic of intense contestation.

Giants, by virtue of their size, accumulate the power to entice and motivate, to destroy and rebuild. Revolutionaries move in absolute terms without much consideration for the fate of those whom they consider an impediment to their radical ideas. There is a lack of grace or subtlety in the abrupt and bulky movements of revolutionary giants. So when Khomeini became embroiled in the revolution in Iran

---

[3] The Constitution of the Islamic Republic of Iran. Retrieved from www.iranchamber.com/government/laws/constitution.php (accessed 12 October 2012).

in 1979, it was inevitable that he would become a divisive figure. He was, after all, under the impression that his was a just battle in support of the oppressed against their oppressors. 'What is important for me is resistance against oppression [*zulm*],' he proclaimed repeatedly. 'I will be wherever this resistance is pursued the best.'[4]

In the light of this dichotomisation of the world into a cosmic battle between justice and evil, the revolution in Iran, like other revolutions before it, created immense fissures. Even when Khomeini was adamant about keeping the unity of the revolutionary forces, when he appealed to the 'various classes of the nation', the students, religious minorities, scholars, professors, judges, civil servants, workers and peasants,[5] and declared himself the brother of all of them, he made clear that attacks by counter-revolutionaries 'club-wielding thugs and other trouble-makers' may result in their killing.[6] Likewise, Khomeini deemed it permissible to kill members of the Iranian armed forces in 'self-defence' if they were directly responsible for the killing of demonstrators against the shah or a major pillar of his regime.[7] If necessary, Khomeini would tolerate and decree death and destruction in order to rescue the revolution from its opponents.

It was in this way that Khomeini's psycho-nationalism in the name of God, Islam, sacrifice, blood and honour created an internal 'other', the counter-revolutionary opponent that needed to be uprooted in order to cleanse the residues of the previous order in a grand effort to recapture a seemingly lost but realistically irretrievable history, in the case of Khomeini and his followers encapsulated in the quest for an 'authentically' Islamic identity for Iran. However, death was not exclusive; it was not only the counter-revolutionary 'other' that was threatened. Comparable to the discourse permeating

---

[4] Ruhollah Khomeini, *Ain-e enghelab-e Islami: Gozidehai az andisheh va ara-ye Imam Khomeini*, Tehran: Moasses-ye tanzim va naschr-e assar-e Imam Khomeini, 1373 [1994], p. 497.
[5] Khomeini, *Islam and Revolution I*, pp. 252–3.
[6] Ibid., p. 248.
[7] Ibid., p. 314.

the other revolutions of modern history – Russian, Cuban, Chinese – the Iranian revolutionaries, too, blurred the boundaries between life and death in order to stress the momentous importance of the struggle at hand. After all, despite the wave of executions that occurred after the revolution, more Iranians supporting Khomeini died than those opposing him, not least in the trenches of the Iran–Iraq war between 1980 and 8. As such, the revolution claimed the lives of both 'self' and 'other', revolutionary and counter-revolutionary, and no Iranian remained untouched by the events. Despite repeated calls for a non-confrontational policy, Khomeini, as indicated, accepted death as an inevitability of the revolutionary process in Iran. Hence the tragedies that he and his followers created for many Iranians. As he proclaimed in an address to the Pope – who tried to mitigate the repercussions of the US embassy takeover by Muslim students supporting Khomeini, including the threat of US military strikes – in November 1979:

> We fear neither military action nor economic boycott, for we are the followers of Imams who welcomed martyrdom. Our people are also ready to welcome martyrdom today . . . We have a population of thirty-five million people, many of whom are longing for martyrdom. All thirty-five million of us would go into battle and after we had all become martyrs, they could do what they liked with Iran. No, we are not afraid of military intervention. We are warriors and strugglers; our young men have fought barehanded against tanks, cannons, and machine guns, so Mr. Carter should not try to intimidate us. We are accustomed to fighting and even when we have lacked weapons, we have had our bodies, and we can make use of them again.[8]

Revolutionaries claim the individual in their entirety. Khomeini was not content to claim the consciousness of Iranians; his discourse also targeted their bodies. As such, the Iranian revolution did not only

[8] Ibid., p. 285.

engender new institutions that had never existed in human history in this shape and form before – a Supreme Jurisprudent (*Vali-e faqih*), a Council of Guardians (*Shoray-e negahban*), an Assembly of Experts (*Shoray-e khebregan*) – but also added to this formal 'macro-sphere' of high politics very immediate 'micro-norms' that were meant to reengineer Iranians within an increasingly Irano-Islamicised system.

Khomeini's vision of governance as a synthesis of religious, moral and political ordinances was not without precedent in Iranian history.[9] Even the ancient kings of Persia, loathed by the revolutionaries because of their association with the ideology of the shah, claimed the guidance of god (*Ahura Mazda*) in their cosmic dealings with their subjects and the world that they so stunningly dominated. But the innovative, if egregious, fusion of republicanism and (Shia) Islam that underpins the Islamic Republic of Iran to the present day is without precedent and did not limit itself to the sphere of high politics or the state. Rather the contrary, in true psycho-nationalist fashion, the revolution, as it was pursued by Khomeini and his followers, reached all the way down to the subjectivity of Iranians. From mundane examples such as the emergence of the beard as a revolutionary symbol, the vilification of ties and miniskirts as manifestations of 'western decadence' and the corruption of Iranian culture under the shah, to substantial and legalised curtailments of individual rights, especially for women, the moralistic discourse offered by Khomeini was not merely premised on political change, it was meant to produce a new, 'ideal' subjectivity for Iranians:

> Governments that do not base themselves on divine law conceive of justice only in the natural realm; you will find them concerned only with the prevention of disorder and not with the moral refinement of the people. Whatever a person does in his own home is of no importance, so long as he causes no disorder in

---

[9] On the making of Iran's constitution, see also Asghar Schirazi, *The Constitution of Iran: Politics and the State in the Islamic Republic* (trans. John O' Kane), London: I.B. Tauris, 1998.

the street. In other words, people are free to do as they please at home. Divine governments, however, set themselves the task of making man into what he should be.[10]

The blind spots of and loopholes in this grand effort to reengineer subjectivity in Iran are obvious, which is why Khomeini's discourse created spaces of dissent and resistance where Iranians attempted to push back the gigantic intrusions into their individual preferences and daily lives by the state. It is within the sphere delineated by approval and rejection where the legacy of Khomeini is contested within Iran and beyond until today. But undoubtedly, Khomeini successfully supervised the institutionalisation of a new form of governance which had not existed in human history before and which survived a devastating eight-year-long war against Saddam Hussein's Iraq, a comprehensive sanctions regime spearheaded by the United States, and continuous military threats by Israel. Not unlike Khomeini himself, the political system in Iran proved itself steely, somewhat stoic and indomitable. Hence, after more than three decades, the Islamic Republic continues to be a contested invention, one that is trotting along with just enough psycho-nationalist vigour to keep the populace in control, but without the confidence to venture beyond the status quo and realise the true potentials of the Iranian idea.[11]

BIOGRAPHICAL TRAJECTORIES

There are a few constants in Khomeini's biography that reveal the tensions in his political thought, which appears, at times, eclectic and paradoxical. How could Khomeini talk about the God-'given right of liberty and freedom' that Islam guarantees and proclaim that 'freedom is the primary right of humans' while also supervising the execution of political prisoners throughout the first decade of

---

[10] Khomeini, *Islam and Revolution I*, p. 330.
[11] See further Arshin Adib-Moghaddam, 'What Is Radicalism: Power and Resistance in Iran', *Middle East Critique*, Vol. 21, No. 1, 2012, pp. 271–90.

the revolution?[12] How could he write love poetry and constrain art and literature in Iran at the same time? What influences affected his political and social attitudes?

Some scholars have taken the short route to explain the tensions in Khomeini's thought. They argue that he was a cynical opportunist. He would say one thing to Iranians in order to secure their support for the revolution and do something else in practice. There is no doubt that Khomeini's utopian vision was implemented with a good deal of Machiavellian pragmatism. He had to navigate within a context that was not really Islamic in the sense in which he interpreted Islam, and was aware that he had to compromise – as he did at the beginning of the revolution – with other forces including the liberal-nationalist *Nehzat-e azadi-ye Iran* (Freedom Movement of Iran), led by the first Prime Minister Mehdi Bazargan, and liberal technocrats such as Abolhasan Bani Sadr, who became the first president of the Islamic Republic.[13] But the adherence to a highly politicised, interest-based and state-centric interpretation of Islam in Iran was also due to his convictions as a cleric, religious scholar and theologian. In many ways, Khomeini was a *mujtahid* (Islamic legal expert) first and a revolutionary second; his radical messages were always also steeped in legalistic premises informed by his interpretation of the Shia tradition of *usul al-fiqh* (principles of Islamic jurisprudence).

As a consequence of that theological outlook, the *ulema* (clerics) occupied a central role in Khomeini's political discourse. In almost all of his major proclamations before, during and after the revolution, he stressed their centrality. For instance, in 1967 in an open letter to the shah's Prime Minister Amir Abbas Hoveyda in which he described them as 'the guardians of the independence and

---

[12] Mohammad-Hossein Jamshidi (ed.), *Andishey-e siasiy-e imam Khomeini*, Tehran: Pajoheshkade-ye imam Khomeini va enghelabe islami, 1384 [2005], pp. 245, 246.

[13] Mehdi Bazargan and his cabinet resigned during the hostage crisis and in protest against Iran's deteriorating human rights situation at the beginning of the revolution. Abolhasan Bani Sadr was dismissed from the presidency in 1981 after being impeached by the Iranian parliament. He fled Iran into exile in 1981.

integrity of the Muslim countries'[14] or in 1971 in a message to the pilgrims in Mecca, when he demeaned their 'oppression' by the shah and foreigners,[15] and their apathy in the face of tyranny which betrayed the legacy of 'Imam Hussein's bloody revolt' against the Umayyad caliph Yazid in the seventh century AD.[16] After his return to Iran in 1979, he supported the involvement of the *mujtahideen* of the newly established 'Revolutionary Council' in the cultural revolution with the aim to 'Islamise' the universities in order 'to make them autonomous, independent of the West and independent of the East [i.e. the Soviet Union]', to establish an 'independent university system and an independent culture'.[17] Undoubtedly, Khomeini gave a special place to what he occasionally referred to as the 'clerical class'.[18]

This should not come as a surprise. The clerical strata of Iranian society were the primary reference point for Khomeini throughout his life. His clerical worldview is one of the few constants that can be drawn from his biography. Surely, if Khomeini had been born an aristocrat tied to the ruling monarchs or into a working-class family, his views on Iranian politics would have been rather different. But his biography made it inevitable that there would emerge a clerical approach to politics, culture and society: he was born Ruhollah Musawi Khomeini on 24 September 1902, into a middle-class clerical family in the small town of Khomein. The family origin of his

---

[14] Khomeini, *Islam and Revolution I*, p. 192.
[15] Ibid., p. 197.
[16] Ibid., p. 205.
[17] Ibid., p. 298.
[18] It was Ayatollah Morteza Mutahhari, one of the closest clerical allies of Khomeini, who was adamant on stressing the centrality of the 'clerical class' to the state and politics in Iran and who used the term even more forcefully in his influential books and talks at the famed Hosseiniyeh Ershad in Tehran, where he lectured together with Ali Shariati before the revolution. Mutahhari and Khomeini were particularly adamant about stressing that clerical leadership superseded intellectual leadership, whereas lay intellectuals such as Shariati were largely opposed to clerical governance. On Shariati, see the splendid book by Ali Rahnema, *An Islamic Utopian: A Political Biography of Ali Shariati*, London: I.B. Tauris, 1998. On Ayatollah Mutahhari and his focus on clerical leadership, see Mahmood T. Davari, *The Political Thought of Ayatollah Murtaza Mutahhari: An Iranian Theoretician of the Islamic State*, London: Routledge, 2005, pp. 134–5.

ancestors was linked to the seventh Imam of the Shia Imam Musa al-Kazim, which identifies the family as 'Musawi Seyyeds' who claim descent from the Prophet Mohammed. His immediate ancestors had immigrated to Iran from Northern India, where they had settled from their original abode in Neishapur in North-Eastern Iran in the early eighteenth century.[19] His grandfather, Seyyed Ahmad Musawi 'Hindi' (literally 'the Indian'), was invited to the town of Khomein by a certain Yusef Khan during pilgrimage to the shrine city of Najaf in Iraq, where Ali, the first Imam of the Shi'i, is buried. Seyyed Ahmad was a contemporary and relative of Mir-Hamed Hossein (d. 1880), who authored several widely distributed volumes on disputes between Sunni and Shi'i in the traditional religious canon.

Khomeini's father Mostafa kept the religious tradition of the family alive and trained as a *mujtahid* first in Isfahan in Iran, and then in the *atabat* (shrine cities) of Samarra and Najaf in Iraq. In March 1903, just five months into Khomeini's life, Mostafa was murdered under disputed circumstances. With such a prominent religious tradition within the family, there was no doubt that Khomeini would pursue the clerical path as well. His education commenced in earnest between 1920 and 1 at the Mirza Yusuf Khan *madrasa* in Arak (previously Sultanabad), which hosted Sheikh Abdolkarim Haeri (d. 1936), one of the most preeminent religious scholars in Iran during that period. At this stage of his studies, Khomeini focused on logic and jurisprudence (*Ja'fari* or *Ithna 'asheri*), and was firmly steeped in the clerical traditions of the day. He continued his studies in jurisprudence, gnosis, ethics, philosophy and semantics at the Dar al-Shafa in Qom, which was the principle centre of religious learning in Iran and a major pilgrimage site due to the Shrine of Hazrat-e Masoumeh, a daughter of Musa al-Kazim (745–99 AD). Khomeini was to forge a career in Qom that spawned four decades (1923–62), over a period

---

[19] See Hamid Algar, 'A Short Biography', in Abdar Rahman Koya (ed.), *Imam Khomeini: Life, Thought and Legacy*, Petaling Jaya: Islamic Book, 2009, p. 19 and Baqer Moin, *Khomeini: Life of the Ayatollah*, London: I.B. Tauris, 1999, p. 2.

that turned him into an influential religious scholar and increasingly vocal political personality.[20]

The methodical lifestyle that Khomeini followed, signposted by praying, studying, lectures and teaching, may explain the discipline that many of his associates and biographers attributed to him. According to one observer, Khomeini adhered to a 'systematic' daily routine, and even followed a particular method in his movements.[21] He would always step 'on the minbar with his left leg first, pause and then commence his sermon'.[22] He would pay particular attention to the behaviour of his students, reminding them that 'discipline and organisation' were central traits that would ensure success in their future lives.[23] The late Sadegh Tabatabai, one of Khomeini's close supporters who accompanied him on the plane on his triumphant return to Tehran on 1 February 1979, adds in his recently published biography that Khomeini followed a careful dress code. In one anecdote, Khomeini made sure that his dark-blue socks matched the grey colour of his cloak, before he went to the mosque.[24] Tabatabai also indicates that Khomeini seemed to be a connoisseur of eau de toilette.[25] Beyond his disciplined demeanour then, there seemed to be whiffs of 'worldliness' to Khomeini's character. At the same time, the 'vaticanic' lifestyle in Qom, compounded by his similarly routinised life in exile in Najaf (1965–78), must have made an indelible imprint on Khomeini, entrenching his clerical world view.

Throughout his life, Khomeini felt more comfortable in the religious confines of his circles and rather anxious about the secular realities encroaching on them. In particular, Qom was his centre of the universe, the imperial Vatican of the Shi'i that was waiting

---

[20] For a recent introduction to Shi'i history and politics, see Hamid Dabashi, *Shi'ism: A Religion of Protest*, Cambridge, MA: Harvard University Press, 2011.
[21] Rouhani (Ziarati), *Baresi va tahlil az nehzate imam Khomeini*, p. 29.
[22] Ibid., p. 30.
[23] Ibid.
[24] Sadegh Tabatabai, *Khaterat-e siasi – ejtemai-ye doktor Sadegh Tabatabai, jelde aval*, vol. i, Tehran: Mo'aseseh-ye chap va nashr-e oruj, 1387 [2008], p. 156.
[25] Ibid., pp. 155–6.

to be awakened to the calls of revolution. The efforts of Khomeini to politicise Qom bore fruit when, in January 1978, demonstrators clashed with the shah's security forces. 'The religious centre in Qom has brought Iran back to life,' he proudly proclaimed from the famed Sheikh Ansari mosque in Najaf. 'The name of the religious centre in Qom will remain inscribed in history for all time. By comparison with Qom, we here in Najaf are dead and buried; it is Qom that has brought Islam back to life.'[26] It should not come as a surprise, then, that after the revolution Khomeini immediately settled in Qom and proclaimed himself a 'proud citizen' of the town.[27] The turbulent period immediately after the establishment of the Islamic Republic necessitated his return to Tehran, but it is not too far-fetched to argue that Khomeini regarded Qom as the real epicentre of religious activism and revolution both in Iran and throughout the Muslim world. Until today, Qom remains the headquarter for the psycho-nationalist discourse sustaining the theological underpinning of the Islamic Republic.

This socialisation of Khomeini into a senior cleric whose world view emerged relatively independent from competing secular institutions was possible because of a functioning institutional infrastructure that abetted the clerical class in Iran at least since the Safavid dynasty (1502–1736), which established Shia-Islam as the country's main national narrative. As I have discussed in Chapter 1, it was under the Safavids, and in particular during the rule of Shah Abbas I (1571–1629), that the idea of Imamite jurisprudence in the Twelver-Shia tradition was institutionalised in the burgeoning *madrasas* and other educational and civic institutions sponsored by the state, which were increasingly populated by senior Shia scholars recruited from all over the Muslim world, in particular from Iraq, Syria and Lebanon. As I have mentioned, these clerics were lead by the aforementioned Muhaqiq al-Karaki (also al-Thani), a pivotal clerical personality who

---

[26] Khomeini, *Islam and Revolution I*, p. 218.
[27] Quoted in Algar, 'A Short Biography', p. 24. In the meantime, the clerical links in his life were reinforced by his marriage to Qods-e Iran Saqafai (or Qodsi) in 1929, the daughter of Ayatollah Mirza Mohammad Saqafi. They were married until Khomeini's death in 1989.

established one of the most powerful refutations of the Sufi tradition in Iran and set the jurisprudential tenets for the predominant authority of the jurist based on the Imamite succession.[28] Therefore, the *usuli* (rationalist) school of Shia Islam became increasingly influential in the seminaries at the expense of the followers of the traditionalist (*akhbari*) paradigm. Al-Karaki emphasised the power of *ijtihad* or dialectical reasoning, and made a strong case in favour of the leadership of *mujtahids* whose divine decrees would be emulated (*taqlid*) by their followers.[29] As indicated, Al-Karaki's reinvention of a Shia orthodoxy based on a religious hierarchy dominated by a supreme jurist can be seen as one of the main precursors to Khomeini's idea of the *Velayat-e faqih* or the rule of the Supreme Jurisprudent. Khomeini, then, lodged into a pre-existent infrastructure of clerical hegemony.

CLERICAL COGNITIONS

My emphasis on a clerical world view needs to be qualified further now, for Khomeini was not merely a *mujtahid* born and raised within a society permeated by a thick fabric of religious norms and institutions, but a revolutionary cleric who rejected some of the same. For sure, no one is born a revolutionary (or a psycho-nationalist for that matter). Indeed, in his first book, *Kashf-e Asrar* (*Discovery of Secrets*), published in 1943, Khomeini did not totally reject the rule of the first Pahlavi monarch Reza Shah when he wrote that a superficial state is better than none at all.[30] Neither was he particularly political during his years in Qom, at least in the initial years, always careful to respect the prevalent hierarchies and the quietist leadership of Ayatollahs Haeri, and Ayatollah Hussein Boroujerdi – Iran's main *marja-e taqlid* from the end of the 1940s until his death in 1961. But *Kashf-e Asrar*, his first major political intervention, is a

---

[28] See further, Rula Jurdi Abisaab, *Converting Persia: Religion and Power in the Safavid Empire*, London: I.B. Tauris, 2004, p. 24. For Karaki's writings, see Muhaqiq al-Karaki, *Jameal maqasid*, vol. 2, Qum: Ahlol Bayt Publication, 1365 [1986].
[29] See further, Amir-Moezzi, *The Divine Guide in Early Shi'ism*, pp. 138–9.
[30] Ruhollah Khomeini, *Kashf-e Asrar*, Qom: Azadi Publications, no date, p. 180.

useful reference point because it unveils three major preferences of Khomeini's political thought that were to play a central role in praxis in the build up to the revolution and after the establishment of the Islamic Republic in 1979.

First, although it is true that in *Kashf-e Asrar* Khomeini did not attack the monarchy in a comparably explicit manner as he did in his lectures and speeches in the 1960s and 1970s, he did, even at this early stage, emphasise the centrality of the clergy to the supervision of any kind of earthly government. In an oft-cited sentence, he proclaimed that he 'does not say that government must be in the hands of the *faqih*'.[31] But this sentence must be read in accordance with the sections where Khomeini attributes absolute sovereignty to God and absolute legitimacy to Islamic governance which is compelled to safeguard implementation of the *shariah*: 'The only government that reason accepts as legitimate and welcomes freely and happily is the government of God, Whose every act is just and Whose right it is to rule over the whole world and all the particles of existence.'[32] At once, Khomeini's schooling in jurisprudence, philosophy and theology stands out when he speaks of governance, reason and religious legitimacy, respectively: 'It is in contrast with the government of God that the nature of all existing governments becomes clear, as well as the sole legitimacy of Islamic government.'[33] The monarchy, and every other form of governance for that matter, is only legitimate for the time being and only if it accepts the sovereignty of God and the legitimate supervision of the religious leaders. It was quite apparent, judging from Khomeini's distaste for the 'court-clerics' who bowed to the shah and the scathing and demeaning tone he reserved for the monarchy itself in *Kashf-e Asrar*, that he was not at all convinced that Reza Shah's state was competent, or even interested in implementing those 'most advanced laws in the world' which would 'lead

---

[31] Khomeini, *Islam and Revolution I*, p. 170.
[32] Ibid.
[33] Ibid.

to the establishment of the Virtuous City'.[34] Psycho-nationalism bestows upon its agent a particularly optimistic arrogance towards history and the 'other' more generally.

The reference by Khomeini to the establishment of the Virtuous City reveals a second aspect that permeates *Kashf-e Asrar*, and which can be identified as another constant in his political thought and praxis: namely, his schooling in and emphasis on philosophy. Terms such as 'reason', 'justice', 'wisdom' and 'oppression' are central to the political discourse of Khomeini throughout his life. They are indicative of his education in *hekmat* (literally, 'wisdom'), and *irfan* ('gnosis'), taught to him by luminaries such as Mirza Mohammad Ali Shahabadi (d. 1950), a scholar of the classical Islamic philosophy of Ibn Sina (Avicenna), Ibn Arabi and Nassir al-Din Tusi.[35] The concept of the Virtuous City denotes an ideal and just polity, and entered political theory in Iran via the Platonic tradition in general and the classical Islamic philosophy of Farabi in particular. Such a utopian 'ideal order', under the aegis of an Iranianised Shia-Islam, was exactly what Khomeini and his followers were striving for in Iran – hence the high costs that this 'heavenly' project extracted from Iranian society.

Khomeini was an ardent student of philosophy, in particular the concept of *vahdat al-vojud* (unity of existence) and *tawheed* (unity of God) – conceptualised by Ibn Sina and Ibn Arabi – and, at a later stage, an enthusiastic lecturer on related themes in the seminaries of Qom.[36] The political aspects of this philosophical tradition in Iran that must have made the greatest impact on Khomeini, judging from the terms and methods permeating his discourse, are the quest for the ideal human being or *insane-e kamel* in Ibn Arabi's words. The development of this ideal human being must be the prime objective of governance of the community and the leadership of the Supreme

---

[34] Ibid.
[35] For a detailed account of the linkage between Ibn Arabi and Khomeini, see Latife Reda Ali, *Khomeini's Discourse of Resistance: The Discourse of Power of the Islamic Revolution*, PhD thesis, London: School of Oriental and African Studies, 2012.
[36] Moin, *Life of the Ayatollah*, pp. 40–41.

Jurisprudent, whose 'exalted' position is not entirely remote from the 'philosopher-king' in the Platonic tradition. So convinced was Khomeini of the superiority of classical Islamic philosophy that he urged the former leader of the Soviet Union – Mikhail Gorbachov – in a letter delivered to him in 1988, to study the Peripatetic philosophy of Farabi and Ibn Sina, the mysticism of Ibn Arabi, the transcendental philosophy of Mulla Sadra and the Ishraqi theosophy of Sohrawardi.[37] Gorbachov politely declined, but according to one Russian scholar, the message was widely distributed in the Soviet Union in the period of its disintegration in 1989–90.[38]

Ultimately, in truly psycho-nationalist fashion, Khomeini the politician and revolutionary eclipsed the abstract, contemplative and partially 'non-Islamic' notions permeating the philosophy of the classical philosophers in favour of a highly utilitarian, theological and power-based interpretation. In the dialectic between philosophy and psycho-nationalist politics, Khomeini opted for the latter, especially in the 1960s when he focused his activities more stringently on combating the policies of the shah. As such, it is not too far-fetched to argue that Ibn Arabi's emphasis on sainthood (*vilaya*) and his designation of the *vali* as a friend of God whose practices and devotion to knowledge of God enable him to claim succession to the Prophet, informed Khomeini's theory of *Velayat-e faqih*. But at the same time, Ibn Arabi and the Sufi tradition inspired by him would have rejected the ideological and positivist certainty that Khomeini attached to the position of the *vali-e faqih* in favour of an individual path towards the 'ideal human being'.[39] Not unlike other Islamists of his generation – Muhammad Ala Mawdudi in the subcontinent, Hassan al-Banna and Sayyid Qutb in Egypt, Ayatollah Mohammad Baqir al-Sadr in Iraq and others – Khomeini forged a particularly hierarchical, masculine

---

[37] Ibid., pp. 274–6.
[38] See Alexander Knysh, 'Irfan Revisited: Khomeini and the Legacy of Islamic Mystical Philosophy', *The Middle East Journal*, Vol. 64, No. 4 (1992), p. 652.
[39] See further, William C. Chittick, *The Sufi Path of Knowledge: Ibn Al-Arabi's Metaphysics of Imagination*, Albany: State University of New York Press, 1989.

and authoritarian interpretation of the role of Islam in politics and society. Eclipsed were the abstract and contemplative ideas of the classical philosophers of the heydays of Muslim empires when Islam was not a contested ideational commodity. Ibn Sina, Farabi and Ibn Arabi did not have to proclaim Islam as the solution at every twist and turn of their discourse exactly because their Muslim identity, and the Islamic legitimation of the polity they lived in, was not threatened.[40] The era of the postcolonial nation-state in the Muslim world changed all of that. It turned Islam into a contested ideational system and a space of immense contestation. Islam, being Muslim, after all, is also about identity, whether it is individual, religious and imperial or – more stringently since the break-up of the Ottoman Empire in the early twentieth century – national. As such, the organisational outfit of infant nation-states, as opposed to the organically grown Islamic confessional empires of yesterday, gave centre stage to issues of governance and sovereignty in a way that was not present before. Enter the idea of a centralised state that would turn Islam at once into a source of legitimacy, sovereignty and psycho-national ideology. In short, in the twentieth century, Islam extended its purview into unchartered territories exactly because it was pasted by Khomeini and others onto the fabric of the modern nation-state, a secular structure for which it has proven to be a loose fit.

Quite from the outset then, and this is the third constant we can distil from *Kashf-e Asrar*, the clerical world view that I have described so far was complemented and radicalised by a profoundly political and state-centric interpretation of the Imamite tradition in Iran. Here as well, Khomeini was a product of a historical dialectic: he lived through a tumultuous period in Iran's history. As a young orphan, he witnessed the tremors of the Constitutional Revolt (1906–11) which established the first parliament in Iran; the subsequent coup d'état by Reza Khan in 1921 which institutionalised the Pahlavi

---

[40] See further, Muhsin S. Mahdi, *Alfarabi and the Foundation of Islamic Political Philosophy*, Chicago: University of Chicago Press, 2010.

dynasty; his deposition by the British in 1941; the MI6/CIA coup d'état which toppled Mohammad Mossadegh in 1953 and reinstated the dictatorship of the second Pahlavi Monarch, Mohammad Reza Shah; and his own revolt against the shah's White Revolution in 1963. In addition to these fluctuations of the sovereignty and legitimacy of the state, and confrontational state–society relations, his was also a period of external domination of Iranian affairs which was exercised by the Russians and British in the early twentieth century, and after the Second World War increasingly by the United States. Khomeini witnessed the shah's dependency on foreign support for its survival and the Pahlavis systematic programme of cultural westernisation (delegated in truly authoritarian fashion from the top down) with awe. When, in 1964, the shah granted legal immunity to US citizens on Iranian territory, Khomeini criticised him with a famous, ironic allegory:

> They have reduced the Iranian people to a level lower than that of an American dog. If someone runs over a dog belonging to an American, he will be prosecuted. Even if the Shah himself were to run over a dog belonging to an American, he would be prosecuted. But if an American cook runs over the Shah, the head of state, no one will have the right to interfere with him.[41]

The political discourse of Khomeini reveals two central themes with regard to the historical context that he was embedded in: a particular emphasis on a strong state, and a profound focus on independence from foreign influences. He was under the firm impression that in the quest for a stable state and independence, especially from the United States, the role of Islam would be pivotal. At least in theory, the Supreme Jurisprudent resembles a Leviathan whose purpose is to secure and stabilise the state and ensure the Islamicity of the system. To that end, Khomeini equipped the state with a dual legitimacy – religious and popular – with the former superseding the latter in terms

---

[41] Khomeini, *Islam and Revolution I*, p. 182.

of importance. The cornerstone of this theory of Islamic governance was that in the absence of the leadership of the Twelfth Imam of the Shia, the so-called 'occultation era', only the 'just jurists' are entitled to the permanent guardianship and governance of Muslim societies. Indeed, from the perspective of Khomeini, no government can be deemed 'reasonable' if it is not based on the 'divine law of God' executed by a 'just and wise governor' who would ensure the stability of the state in the absence of the superior leadership of the Imams.[42] As he wrote in *Kashf-e Asrar*, undoubtedly with Reza Shah in mind, 'Reason can never accept that a man who is no different from others in outward or inward accomplishments, unless he is maybe inferior to them, should have his dictates considered proper and just and his government legitimate, merely because he has succeeded in gathering around himself a gang to plunder the country and murder its people.'[43] Given that absolute sovereignty and absolute legitimacy is attributed to God and his divine law (*shariah*),[44] and that only the *mujtahideen* and – primus inter pares – the Supreme Jurisprudent have acquired superior knowledge of the political and religious criteria to establish an Islamic government, it is they who should be in charge of the guardianship of society.[45] In fact, they would lead the *umma* as representatives of the 'infallible imams'. As such, any other form of governance is deemed 'usurping'[46] and an interference in the sovereignty of God.[47] In this way, the Islamic Republic added a theocratic element to the psycho-nationalist pathologies of contemporary Iranian politics.

At the same time, the *Vali-e faqih* does not merely claim divine sovereignty on behalf of the Islamic state, for he is also bound to

---

[42] Ruhollah Khomeini, *Shou'n va Ekhtiyarate Valiye Faqih*, Tehran: Vezarat-e Ershade Islami, 1986, pp. 29–30.
[43] Khomeini, *Islam and Revolution I*, p. 169.
[44] Ruhollah Khomeini, *Al Makaseb al Muharrama*, vol. ii, Tehran: The Institute for Compilation and Publication of Imam Khomeini's Work, 1995, p. 160.
[45] Ruhollah Khomeini, *Sahifeh-ye Iman (Sahifeh-ye Nur, vol. x): An Athology of Imam Khomeinis Speeches, Messages, Interviews, Decrees, Religious Permissions, and Letters*, Tehran: The Institute for Compilation of Imam Khomeini's Works, 2008, p. 308.
[46] Khomeini, *Sahifeh-ye Imam, vol. xi*, p. 403.
[47] Khomeini, *Al Makaseb al Muharrama, vol. ii*, p. 160.

public accountability. According to Khomeini, political leadership that is not based on the acceptance of the populace must be deemed illegitimate, even if it is 'righteous'.[48] Ultimately then, he and his followers equipped the Islamic state in Iran with a dual prophylaxis against destabilisation. On the one hand, a sanctified legitimacy, on the other, a popular one: the Leviathan that Khomeini approved as the head of state in Iran is distinctly Janus-faced, attached to a 'sanctified' corpus and to a democratised underbelly. Until today, the Islamic Republic has not managed to bridge the intrinsic contradictions that this system provokes. Khomeini did not enter the revolution with an assured plan to institutionalise his theory of governance. He was, after all, a product of the revolutionary process that was driven by the Iranian people on the streets in their battles against the security forces of the shah. But when Iranians finally overthrew the monarchy in 1979, Khomeini was catapulted into the position of leadership, which he and his followers used in order to implement their vision of an ideal, Shia-Islamic order in Iran.

Certainly, for the hundreds of thousands who mourned the death of their 'Imam' on 3 June 1989, Khomeini, who had convulsed their generation with such awesome vigour, would be remembered with an unbridled passion. Their chant, 'Azast azast emrooz ruze azaast emrooz Khomeini-e bot shekan sahabe azast emrooz', raised Khomeini almost to a prophetic status, likening the importance of his revolt to the smashing of the idols by the Prophet Mohammad in Mecca. Khomeini had seduced, in an unmistakably charismatic manner, a generation of Iranians whose rage and trepidation against the shah caused one of the most earth-shattering revolutionary tremors of modernity. More than two decades after his death, the glow of the founder of the Islamic Republic suffuses all leaders of post-revolutionary Iran, and his legacy remains hotly debated, both inside the country and among the Iranian diaspora. There is no doubt that his persona continuous to elicit strong reactions, both among his

---

[48] Khomeini, *Sahifeh-ye Imam*, vol. v, p. 244.

loyal followers and among his detractors: to many, his central role in the establishment of the Islamic Republic was an act of political genius; to many others it was an act of ultimate betrayal.

AFTER KHOMEINI IS BEFORE KHOMEINI

It is the nature of giants to attract tall narratives. In Iran, there continues to exist a virtual 'Khomeini industry', a range of publishing houses and foundations that continuously produce books and studies about him that are distributed in several languages throughout the Muslim world and beyond. Khomeini's portrait can be found on Iran's currency, pictures of him adorn buildings on the inside and outside and there are several web pages dedicated to his legacy, including on social networking sites such as Facebook. As we have seen in the previous chapters, psycho-nationalism is cognitively intrusive exactly because it is professionally engineered by the state and administered by institutions and several connected strata of society with access to state power. The reproduction of Khomeini as a 'national icon' with global appeal is central to present politics in Iran. Official numbers are hard to come by, but there are at least 250,000 studies published in Iran about Khomeini.[49] His tomb, which is located between Tehran and Qom near Iran's national cemetery Behesht-e Zahra (Paradise of Zahra), has been turned into a pilgrimage site and cultural centre headed by his grandson Hassan, whose political persuasion is very close to the reformist factions who want to democratise Iran's theocratic institutions.[50] It was recently linked to Tehran's sprawling metro network and is strategically situated along one of Iran's main highways leading up to the capital. Built in 1989 on a 5,000-acre

---

[49] *Fars News Agency*, 12.03.1386 [2007]. Retrieved from www.farsnews.com/newstext.php?nn=8603110187 (accessed 12 August 2012).

[50] Two granddaughters of Khomeini, namely Zahra Eshraghi and Naiemeh Eshraghi – two ardent Facebook users – have repeatedly expressed their support for the reformist demands for democracy and human rights in Iran. Both have launched campaigns against the compulsory veiling of women. For a recent, comprehensive overview of women's voices in Iran, see Tara Povey and Elaheh Rostami-Povey (eds.), *Women, Power and Politics in 21st Century Iran*, Farnham: Ashgate, 2012.

development which continues to be tinkered with to date, the site is referred to as Haram-e Motahhar or 'sacred shrine'. Khomeini's sarcophagus (and that of his son, Ahmad Khomeini) is placed in a glass chamber with a polished metal-grilled enclosure and is encircled by eight massive marble columns and several more slender columns which support the space-frame ceiling and the gilded dome that overarches the structure. Equipped with polished marble floors and walls on the inside, the exterior of the shrine, with its golden dome and four slender minarets, makes it immediately visible from afar. There is then a well-framed Khomeini iconography in Iran, which continuously reproduces 'Khomeinism' as psycho-nationalism.[51]

What are some of the current effects of this legacy on the institution of the Supreme Leader? The history of the institutionalisation of the role of the supreme jurisprudent has been thoroughly examined and well-documented by many scholars.[52] According to a detailed study of Asghar Shirazi, for instance, the governmental system in Iran can be best described as a hierocracy that 'has separated itself from the traditional religious foundations of legitimation which it had originally emphasized without finding new foundations which it can convincingly define and relate to the *Shari'a* that is to say, to Islam'.[53] Shirazi is right to argue that there has been a shift in the way power is legitimated in Iran, but he (like many others) adheres to a problematic dichotomy between religion (Islam) and modernity when he argues that the 'only relationship the legalists have been able to create between their conception of Islam and the products of modern civilizations is reactive'.[54]

At least since the emergence of the revivalist discourse of Islam in the late nineteenth century, pioneered by luminaries such

---

[51] On the term 'Khomeinism', see further, Ervand Abrahamian, *Khomeinism: Essays on the Islamic Republic*, Berkeley: University of California Press, 1993.
[52] See among others Said Amir Arjomand, *The Turban for the Crown: The Islamic Revolution in Iran*, Oxford: Oxford University Press, 1989.
[53] Asghar Shirazi, *The Constitution of Iran*, p. 304.
[54] Ibid., p. 302.

as Muhammad Abduh and Jamal-ad din Afghani (Asadabadi), modernities and Islams have been engaged in an intense dialectic, which has not been resolved in favour of one or the other.[55] Muslim societies have modernised Islam and Islamicised modernity, as exemplified by the globalisation – institutional and ideational – of Islamic symbols in contemporary metropolises such as Paris, London, Berlin and New York. There has never been a single, western modernity separate from other discourses, much as there has never been a monolithic, unitarian Islam unaffected by other events in global history, whether in Iran or elsewhere: Islams are as hybridised by global history as any other ideational system.[56]

If anything, the contemporary history of Iran is a very good example of overlapping temporalities or modernities that are constantly competing with each other – Islamic, Persian, Western, Shia and Zoroastrian, to name a few. The shah tried to resolve this never-ending dialectic in favour of a Persianised temporal space as discussed. His decision to change the Islamic solar *hejra* calendar into an imperial one in 1976 is emblematic of the Persian-centric ideology that his state espoused. Suddenly, Iran was in the year 2535 based on the presumed date of the foundation of the Achaemenid dynasty, a brazen effort to create a new historical space and meaning for Iran that was not centred on the Islamic *hejra* calendar. After all, in the political imagination of the shah, Iranians were meant to be first and foremost 'Aryan' and racially different from the 'Semitic' Arabs and 'their' Islamic history.

The Islamic Republic reversed these efforts and re-Islamicised the temporal space onto which their Iran was pasted. At the time of writing, Iran is in the year 1395, following the solar *hejra* calendar which begins on the vernal equinox in accordance with astronomical calculations. Consequently, the Iranian New Year (*Nowrouz*, literally

---

[55] I am using the term 'Islams' because there is no all-encompassing consensus on the meaning of 'Islam' in the social and political realm. Islam is what people make of it.
[56] Ibid. See also Ali Mirsepassi, *Political Islam, Iran and the Enlightenment: Philosophies of Hope and Despair*, Cambridge: Cambridge University Press, 2010.

'new day'), which is replete with Zoroastrian symbolism, always falls on the March equinox. At the same time, the first year is fixed around the migration to Medina of the prophet Muhammad in 622 CE. The point of this foray into the way 'Irans'[57] have been dated is to show that the idea of the country and the corresponding invention of identities for Iranians are not processed in a vacuum. The history of the country is as polluted and hybrid as that of any other.

This hybridity manifests itself in the institution of the supreme jurisprudent as well. The idea of the *faqih* as a central institution of the state was invented within the ideational fabric undergirding contemporary notions of the meaning of Iran and how the country should be governed. As such, the idea of the *Velayat-e faqih* is an expression of the historical vicissitudes that enveloped the historical consciousness of an influential segment of the clerical strata of society; it cannot be treated merely as an invention of Khomeini's politics, for he himself was the product of historical circumstances and educational influences that shaped his understanding of the realities in Iran and the world. Consequently, the concept of the *Velayat-e faqih* is replete with diverse residues of Iran's intellectual trajectories as indicated.

The clerical mandate to rule, which was inscribed so vehemently in the Iranian constitution by Khomeini and his followers, was never without its critics. At the beginning of the revolution, leading Shi'i authorities – in Iraq, Ayatollahs Khoi and Sistani, in Lebanon, Ayatollah Fadlallah, and in Iran itself, Ayatollahs Shariatmadari and Qomi – were opposed to the direct clerical leadership of the state espoused by Khomeini and his followers. Ali Rahnema meticulously demonstrates how at the beginning of the revolution there was no real consensus on the inclusion of the *faqih* between the various forces comprised in the provisional government and the Revolutionary Council which was mandated to draft the constitution.[58]

[57] The term 'Irans' is meant to illustrate that there are many interpretations of the meaning of the country and that there is no consensus on the idea of Iran.
[58] Ali Rahnema, 'Ayatollah Khomeini's Rule of the Guardian Jurist: From Theory to Practice', in Arshin Adib-Moghaddam (ed.), *A Critical Introduction to Khomeini*, Cambridge: Cambridge University Press, 2014, pp. 88–114.

Yet, in the final analysis, Khomeini remained the point of fixation of the masses and most revolutionary parties – when he manoeuvred, the nascent political system tilted in his direction. Whereas the liberal and leftist factions were increasingly paralysed in their decision-making and harassed by their Islamist competitors, the elevated position of Khomeini provided him and his followers with the opportunity to inscribe the rule of the supreme jurisprudent into the political process and to put the *faqih*-centred constitution of a posited 'Islamic Republic' to a referendum, which was approved by 98.2 per cent of the electorate. Khomeini was actively positioned, and positioned himself, at the helm of the state until his death in 1989 and his formal and informal powers far outweighed that of any other institution of the Islamic Republic.

Despite the clear absence of a clerical consensus about the role of the *faqih*, at the beginning of the revolution Khomeini was flanked by leading sources of emulation (*marja-e taghlid*) such as Ayatollahs Golpayegani and Mar'ashiye-Najafi. In contrast, the ranks of the major Ayatollahs surrounding the successor of Khomeini, Ali Khamenei, appear scattered, if not depleted. It is too far-fetched to imply that 'today, there is not a single grand Ayatollah in power' as Olivier Roy does,[59] but it is true that Ali Khamenei does not possess the religious legitimacy originally associated with the position of the *faqih*. His power is religiously stunted; it does not reach into the labyrinthine spaces in Qom (and much less into the *howzas* of Najaf, Karbala and Kazimiyah) which are guarded by senior Ayatollahs who operate largely independently from the politics of Tehran.

While in 1979 psycho-nationalism in Iran was infused with a distinctly utopian-Islamic revolutionary passion, personified by the charismatic and populist leadership of Ayatollah Khomeini, today psycho-nationalism in Iran is professionalised, sober and

---

[59] Olivier Roy, *The Failure of Political Islam*, trans. Carole Volk, Cambridge, MA: Harvard University Press, 1996, p. 180.

pragmatic. If Khomeini was the philosopher-imam with the aura of an uncompromising clerical revolutionary whose ideas were steeped in the metaphysics of the imamate tradition in Iran, the current Supreme Leader, Ali Khamenei, seems more like the technocratic CEO of a hyperactive multinational company. Whereas Khomeini took full advantage of his powerful position, both as a revolutionary and as a religious leader, Khamenei has relied far more on the political power that the office of supreme leader bestows upon him. If Khomeini could afford to move radically, Khamenei tends to tip-toe. The differences can be illustrated with a set of interrelated key words that characterise the sources of power exercised by the two leaders:

> Khomeini ↔ revolution ↔ imam ↔ radical change;
> Khamenei ↔ consolidation ↔ prefect ↔ conservatism.

Hence, the power of the state in Iran, devoid of its original revolutionary fervour, reveals itself in an increasingly secularised space where religious norms follow realist policies and where the interest of the system supersedes consensus building among the religious authorities of the country. In 1979, Iran produced a revolutionary-utopian momentum whereas today it is producing a realist-technocratic one. Khomeini himself consciously contributed to this process shortly before his death when he favoured Khamenei over Ayatollah Montazeri as his successor as *vali-e faqih*, which necessitated a central constitutional amendment in 1989.

The constitution stipulates that the supreme jurisprudent must be 'brave', 'upright', 'pious' and an expert of Islam with an excellent understanding of current affairs and the requirements of leading the Islamic state. Chapter 1 of the constitution clarifies the 'fundamental principles' of that leadership further. In Article 2, it is emphasised that the Islamic system in Iran is based on the principle of 'continued *ijtehad* by qualified jurists'. Article 5 adds that the *faqih* (or a council of jurists, *fuqaha*) has the legitimate right to rule during the occultation of the 12th imam of the Shi'i (Imam Mahdi). Article 57 sets out that the *vali-e faqih* is responsible for the supervision of the three branches of the government and Article 110 specifies that this supervisory role includes appointing the jurists to the Guardian Council and the highest judicial authority, holding the position of commander-in-chief with wide-ranging powers to appoint and dismiss the highest echelons of the military leadership, and confirming the presidency.

The power of the *vali-e faqih* to appoint six jurists of the twelve-member Guardian Council is particularly central because the Council is mandated to veto bills by the legislature if they do not 'comply' with Islamic tenets (as interpreted by the Council's members). The Guardian Council also vets the candidates for the presidency, the Parliament (*majlis*) and the Assembly of Experts, which is composed of *mojtaheds* and charged with supervising, electing and removing the supreme leader, if he proves to be unfit for office. More importantly, before the constitutional amendments of 1989, Article 109 of the constitution set out that the *faqih* had to hold the rank of *marja-e taghlid* (or source of emulation), the highest clerical rank in the Shi'i hierarchy. At the time of his appointment as Khomeini's successor, Khamenei was a mid-ranking *hojatol-islam va muslimin*. As president of the Islamic Republic he had demonstrated political competency, the second pillar of the requirement for the *faqih*, but he was not a leading Ayatollah – his religious credentials did not match those of Ayatollah Montazeri, the designated successor to Khomeini. In order to pave the way for his ascendancy to the role of the supreme leader, the requirement of *marjaiyat* had to be dropped from the constitution. This was a major factor in the transformation of the discourse of psycho-nationalism in Iran which, by necessity, tilted away from its original religious-revolutionary emphasis towards a rather more worldly and pragmatist syntax.

FROM THE IMAM TO THE PREFECT

There is no suggestion here that the psycho-nationalist politics exercised by Khomeini were inherently religious. True, the way they were legitimated was firmly rooted in an Islamicised discourse with distinctly Shia connotations, but that doesn't mean that power itself can ever be religious or metaphysical. Power is secular. It is physical, steeped in the dialectic between the ruler and the ruled. In power there is no mediating otherworldly figure exactly because power is exercised immediately, it is not remote; it is penetrative, real and promiscuous.[60] So what shifted was not the secularity of power itself, but the religious claim according to which the sovereignty of the *faqih* was legitimated. This change was necessary, if not inevitable, because of the lack of religious credentials of Khamenei at the time of his appointment as supreme leader in 1989.

In accordance with this circumscribed religious legitimacy and the constitutional amendments implemented, Khamenei has been forced to accept that the institution of the *marja* must retain its relative independence from the office of the *faqih*, at least in the domestic realm in Iran where it has to compete with the powerful clerics concentrated in Qom. Accordingly, Khamenei acknowledges on his official web page the presence of enough *mojtaheds* in Iran to delegate the religious affairs of pious Muslims in the country without impingement by him. 'Therefore those who insist that I publish *risalah* [practical rulings] should pay attention,' he emphasizes.[61] 'This is why I refuse the responsibility of being *marj'a*. Thanks to Allah, there are others. Then, it is not needed.'[62] At the same time, Khamenei claims *marjaiyat* in international affairs. According to him the situation outside Iran is different:

> What is the reason? It is because, if I do not burden myself with it, [the *marjaiyat*] will be lost. The day, on which I feel they – the mujtahids who are available in Qom . . . can afford its burden outside Iran as well, I [will] also go away. Today, I accept the request of Shias outside Iran, as there is no alternative. It is, like

---

[60] See Arshin Adib-Moghaddam, *On the Arab Revolts and the Iranian Revolution*.
[61] Ali Khamenei, 'Biography'. Available at www.leader.ir/langs/en/index.php?p=bio (accessed 21 March 2013).
[62] Ibid.

other cases, of necessity. However, regarding inside Iran, there is no need. The Holy Imam-e Asr [Twelfth Imam of the Shi'i believed to be in occultation] protects and witnesses hawzahs, supports great scholars and guides marjas and people here. I ask Allah to make this phase a blessed one for the Iranian nation as well.[63]

The emphasis on pragmatism is apparent here. Apart from the symbolic last sentence, Khamenei legitimates his *marjaiyat* in international affairs mainly through pragmatism: he 'has to do it' because as the head of the state he has privileged access to the necessary resources. If he doesn't do it, Khamenei seems to claim, the leadership of the Shi'i will be lost to others outside of Iran because 'there is no alternative'. The decision has to be made by 'necessity' in order to safeguard the interest (*maslahat*) of the *umma* in general and 'the Iranian nation' in particular. Khamenei seemed to be aware from the outset that he was appointed out of necessity, not out of preference – that he was the pragmatic option. As he declared upon his inauguration in 1989: 'I am an individual with many faults and shortcomings and really a minor seminarian. Yet, a responsibility has been placed on my shoulders and I will use all my capabilities and all my faith in the Almighty in order to be able to bear this heavy responsibility.'[64]

Of course, the state used its privileged access to the instruments of discipline and punishment, despite the seemingly humble declarations that Khamenei would respect the *marjaiyat* of the senior Ayatollahs. His stand-off with Grand Ayatollah Montazeri in 1997 is a good example. Montazeri repeatedly questioned the

---

[63] Ibid. In order to explain this particular issue further the following section is added:

> The Leader's refusal of the responsibility of becoming marji' for the people in the Islamic Republic of Iran, does not mean that the people inside the country are not allowed to follow him as a marji'. Consequently, multitudes of letters containing questions about religious issues come from inside the country and from abroad. Besides, a very large number of the noble people in Iran have selected the Supreme Leader as their marji'. There was a pressing in addition to the constant pleading by many great figures.

[64] Speech given on Iran's national television, 6 June 1989.

religious credentials of Khamenei and in 1997 published an open letter challenging his religious qualifications to rule as supreme leader. Subsequently, he was put under house arrest until January 2003, when he was allowed to resume his classes on *fiqh* (Islamic theology) in Qom. Yet at the same time, and despite occasional campaigns to project his authority, Khamenei has had to move cautiously around the clerical establishment in Iran; he could never really afford to provoke the higher echelons of the clerical hierarchy in the way Khomeini occasionally dared to. It is interesting, for instance, that Khamenei did not facilitate the house arrest of Ayatollahs Sa'anei and Dastgheib, even as they loudly supported the opposition during the heydays of the reformist 'Green Movement' in 2009. When Khamenei went to Qom to a muted response by the clerical establishment, Dastgheib challenged his authority from Shiraz in a strikingly forthright manner. According to him, the power of supreme leadership had to be confined if the person is not a *marja-e taghlid*. Dastgeib has been a member of the Assembly of Experts for two decades now. During the massive crackdown on protests after the re-election of President Ahmadinejad in 2009, he circulated an open letter among the assembly members criticising the handling of the crisis by Khamenei. 'It is not right', Dastgheib maintained in the letter, 'for one person to be in charge of the country.'[65] In addition, he called an emergency meeting of the Assembly of Experts. Subsequently, his students in Shiraz were harassed, his website was shut down and there were attacks on the Ghoba mosque where Dastgheib has led Friday Prayers for over four decades now. Reassured by the support of most members in the Assembly of Experts, Khamenei dismissed calls for the expulsion of Dastgheib from the Assembly, deeming it – in truly managerial fashion – not 'very appropriate' to do so.[66]

[65] 'Khamenei Challenged by Senior Cleric', *Asia Times Online*, 2 November 2010. Available at www.atimes.com/atimes/Middle_East/LK02Ak02.html (accessed 11 November 2012).
[66] Ibid.

Khamenei has repeatedly acted as a 'prefect' of Ayatollah Khomeini's legacy, rather than a leader in his own right. Exactly because he was not a *marja* when he was appointed supreme leader in 1989, his psycho-nationalism and the power contained therein has relied upon 'managerial' themes. A quick perusal of the major speeches on his official web page shows that apart from occasional references to Islamic imagery and symbols, usually slotted in at the beginning and the end of the speeches, there is an overwhelming emphasis on functional issues of the state. Terms and themes such as leadership, management, reconstruction, security and national development clearly dominate.

In an address to young army cadets at the Imam Ali military academy in December 2005, for instance, Khamenei reminds them that 'military training, observing military discipline, boosting faith and determination' are their major duties.[67] In November 2005, on the occasion of the anniversary of Imam Ali, the first imam of the Shia and the son-in-law of the Prophet Mohammad, Khamenei is equally intent on stressing raison d'état when he cautions that the officials should ensure that there 'is no bribery, administrative corruption, enjoyment of undeserved privileges, waste of working time, disregard for the people, desire to make a fortune . . . and no embezzlement of public funds'.[68] In a speech to the residents of Eastern Azerbaijan in February 2007, he addresses the 'youngsters' who 'have become aware of their inherent worth and merit and are looking for scientific knowledge and new discoveries'.[69] In a clear reference to the recurrent theme of national development, Khamenei stresses that 'they are seeking to tread the path to the high summits of progress'.[70] Determined

---

[67] 'Leader's Address to Army Cadets at Imam Ali Military Academy'. Available at www.leader.ir/langs/en/index.php?p=bayanat&id=3488 (accessed 12 April 2013).
[68] 'Leader's Statement at the Tehran Friday Prayers', 19 August 2005. Available at www.leader.ir/langs/en/index.php?p=bayanat&id=3476 (accessed 19 March 2013).
[69] 'Leader's Speech to the Residents of the Eastern Azarbaijan Province', 17 February 2007. Available at www.leader.ir/langs/en/index.php?p=bayanat&id=3595 (accessed 12 April 2013).
[70] Ibid.

to remind his audience about the development that Iran has already accomplished, he reiterates in typical fashion that Iran 'benefits from abundant talented human resources that are capable of making considerable progress in various areas of activities, and it is up to government officials to make proper use of these valuable resources'.[71] Elsewhere, Khamenei appears more like a minister of education than a supreme leader when he 'encourage[s] academics and the officials in charge of universities [to] promote self-confidence among university students. We should have confidence in our national resources and cultural heritage.'[72] He adds:

> We should determine the country's needs and scientific priorities and base our educational plans on these two factors. Research and thorough investigation may reveal a number of priorities in the humanities, fundamental sciences, and various areas of experimental sciences. The results of these investigations must be taken into account when doing large-scale planning. Due to the limited amount of resources available and the large number of needs we currently have in the country, we should not spend our time on low-priority projects. Neither should we use our human and financial resources in these cases.[73]

This is psycho-nationalism in a distinctly pragmatist garb. When theological themes are touched upon, they are subordinated to the interest of the system in order to deal with the 'complicated economic, financial, political and social problems' facing Muslims today: 'Pundits who enjoy enormous capabilities in Islamic jurisprudence and who have a modern perspective on the current issues must rely on Islamic jurisprudence and its various aspects and double their attempts to

---

[71] Ibid.
[72] 'Supreme Leader's Address to Academics', 24 September 2008. Available at www.leader.ir/langs/en/index.php?p=bayanat&id=4058 (accessed 11 April 2013).
[73] Ibid.

clarify different issues and meet these new requirements.'[74] In his emphasis on the interest (*maslahat*) of the system, Khamenei follows the lead of his mentor Ayatollah Khomeini; in particular towards the end of his life Khomeini enshrined *maslahat* even more firmly as the principle of the state superseding religious ordinances including the first principles of Islam.[75] Indeed, Khomeini personally reprimanded Khamenei in 1987 when the latter was president, reminding him that the state is the most important of God's ordinances and that it can suspend even central commandments of Islam such as prayer, fasting or pilgrimage. Khomeini spoke with the full force of his religious and political authority in a way that Khamenei never really did as supreme leader. Addressing Khamenei, he said:

> From your comments during the Friday prayers it would appear that you do not believe it is correct [to characterize] the state as an absolute trusteeship which God conferred upon the noble Prophet, God bless him and his family and grant them salvation, and that the state is the most important of God's ordinances and has precedence over all other derived ordinances of God. Interpreting what I have said to mean that the state [only] has its powers within the framework of the ordinances of God contradicts my statements. If the powers of the state were [only] operational within the framework of the ordinances of God, the extent of God's sovereignty and the absolute trusteeship given to the prophet would be a meaningless phenomenon devoid of content.[76]

---

[74] 'Hundreds of Ulama, Scholars, Clergymen, and Theology Students of Yazd Province Call on the Leader', 2 January 2008. Available at www.leader.ir/langs/en/index.php?p=bayanat&id=3659 (accessed 8 April 2013).

[75] The Expediency Council entrenched the *maslahat* principle even further. It is mandated to arbitrate disputes between the elected parliament and the Guardian Council in favour of the interest (and stability) of the system. These institutional changes demonstrate the importance of regime survival in the doctrines of the Islamic Republic. This is, of course, in tune with the interest of any other state.

[76] Quoted in Shirazi, *The Constitution of Iran*, p. 230.

Such psycho-nationalism in the name of the divine sovereignty of the state was emblematic of the era of Khomeini and never really returned in this form after his death. It was the particular historical juncture in Iran that allowed him to speak with such immense authority and lent itself to equating the power of the Iranian state with the holiest tenets of (Shia) Islam. Aged eighty-five in 1987, and towards the end of the exhausting eight-year war with Saddam Hussein's Iraq, challenged by domestic upheaval and international isolation, for Khomeini the politician the stability of the Islamic Republic must have been pivotal, hence his increasingly pragmatic discourse of power which fed into a rather more technocratic trend of psycho-nationalism in Iran.

When Khomeini was supreme leader, he was leading a young state with nascent bureaucratic structures and a diffuse political system without much institutional depth. Today, by contrast, Khamenei is at the helm of a state that is far more professionalised, with a rather more differentiated and experienced underbelly, and an inflated public sector that is financially tied to the bureaucracy sustaining the state. Today, then, psycho-nationalism in Iran is introjective; it is disseminated through various channels in order to assault the cognition of the populace. In this process, Khamenei cannot afford to be arbitrary in the way Khomeini could. His movements have to be measured and strategic. His power is channelled through the diverse anchors scattered around the Iranian body politic from the nodal point of the *beit-e imam* in Tehran and from there to a whole cast of powerful loyalists: 'representatives of the imam' at universities, ministries and councils, the editors of the two major national newspapers, *Keyhan* and *Etelaat*, in addition to larger institutions that zigzag through Iran's political system, such as the heads of the economically powerful foundations, the director of the national radio and television network, the Baseej voluntary forces and the Islamic Revolutionary Guard Corps. The latter has become central to the economic and political power sustaining the Islamic Republic in general and the power of the *faqih* in particular.

At the same time, the office of the leader continues to be an institution in the competitive political market in Iran that has to be promoted with its own sophisticated public relations machinery, like a commodity to be sold to a sceptical constituency who are exposed to the competing ideas of influential dissenters, as we will explore more fully in the next chapter.[77] As a consequence of this pluralistic space that continuously impinges on his sovereignty and legitimacy, Khamenei seems to have chosen to rule as a 'prefect' of an unrealised revolutionary dream.

---

[77] See further Arshin Adib-Moghaddam, 'The Pluralistic Momentum in Iran and the Future of the Reform Movement', *Third World Quarterly*, Vol. 27, No. 4 (2006), pp. 665–74.

5 Un-national Therapy: Freedom and Its Discontents

In the previous chapters, I have covered different sites where psycho-nationalist tropes reveal themselves and I have attempted to specify how and why they feed into forms of power, sovereignty and legitimacy which underpin the infrastructure of any contemporary nation-state. I have also begun to show that psycho-nationalism doesn't work, in the sense that it creates too many 'others', in terms of both domestic politics and foreign relations. I have termed the counter-conducts that emanate from this process of exclusion 'psycho-therapeutic' resistance because they too are concerned with bio-political themes, in particular 'identity'. I have already discussed the resistance to the Shah of intellectuals such as Ali Shariati and Jalal al-e Ahmad. This chapter will demonstrate further that centuries of psycho-nationalism in Iran has created certain forms of psycho-therapeutic resistance that oscillate around the question of 'freedom', which has been at the heart of the Iranian quest for democracy, human rights and pluralism for over a century now.

The meaning of 'freedom' in Iran cannot be unravelled exclusively from an 'Islamic' perspective of course. At the same time, liberal concepts and the idea of freedom itself repeatedly have figured prominently in the writings of leading Islamic theoreticians and philosophers in the country. In order to give a brief overview of these ideas and the debates they have provoked, this chapter will follow three steps. Firstly, it will show that the idea of freedom has been at the heart of political events in modern Iran. I will start by sketching some of the major political upheavals in the country, with a particular emphasis on the events surrounding the revolution of 1979. In a second step, I will look at the nexus between Islam and liberal ideas in the political philosophy of major contemporary Iranian thinkers.

And thirdly, I will sketch some of their flaws with a short philosophical critique. In all of this, I do not start with a strict definitional yardstick to measure complex concepts such as liberalism, democracy or freedom. Rather, I attempt to sketch how these concepts are handled within an Iranian and Islamic framework, acknowledging that they are defined by context and historical circumstances. The freedom to carry arms in many parts of the United States seems irresponsible to most Europeans. The freedom to smoke Marijuana in Amsterdam may be considered too liberal elsewhere. Of course, there are norms and rights that might be shared universally by most societies, but it is really the nuances and margins, the grey zones, if you like, that interest me. To that end, I am refraining from starting with an *a priori* definition of freedom, democracy or liberalism, in order that that the sites of my analysis can speak for themselves.

OF IMPERIALISM AND RESISTANCE

What makes the Iranian case so pertinent is that the Islamic revolution of 1979 continues to be constructed and reinvented. Beyond the pragmatism that the humdrum affairs of governance demand, there is no consensus in Iran about the core tenets of the revolution, either within the state or in society as a whole. The issue of freedom particularly is contested. Consequently, what has happened since the establishment of the Islamic Republic in 1979 is a struggle to define the revolution and its position in Iranian history. A diverse range of intellectuals, students, workers, women's rights activists and members of the Iranian state has contested the polity that emerged. Hence there have been recurrent spells of upheaval, the discourse of reform and recurrent mass demonstrations in favour of change.[1] What we have witnessed, in short, is a struggle for the meaning of the Islamic revolution, a struggle that is framed in terms of freedom from the

---

[1] On the history of democracy in Iran, see Fakhreddin Azimi, *The Quest for Democracy in Iran: A Century of Struggle against Authoritarian Rule*, Cambridge, MA: Harvard University Press, 2010.

authority of the state on the one side, and from foreign dictates on the other. As such the revolution is a continuation of Iran's historical quest for representative government and for independence.[2]

Islamic symbols, imagery and norms, moulded and reconstructed in accordance with historical necessity and Iran's political culture, repeatedly were employed in order to articulate this quest for freedom. There was certainly no exclusively 'Islamic' narrative to establish a freer society. Islam in Iran (as anywhere else) has been invented and reconstructed in close dialogue with political, economic, cultural and sociological realities on the ground.[3] True, in the popular imagination in the 'west', Islam continues to be the antithesis to liberal ideas. If the 'west' represents feminism, democracy, freedom of speech and religious tolerance, the Muslim world regularly is represented as inherently misogynistic, homophobic, authoritarian and antagonistic. However, the political thought of the figures I will discuss seems to indicate that Islam could be a recipe for dictatorship as much as a blueprint for liberalism, pluralism and democracy, depending on how the canon is interpreted. For example, Islam can be revolutionary, as in the political thought of Ayatollah Ruhollah Khomeini, or it can be liberal and democratic as in the writings of Abdolkarim Soroush, Mohsen Kadivar, Hasan Eshkevari and others, which I will discuss below. In fact, Islam can be turned into a formula for psycho-nationalism *or* a philosophy accentuating freedom. Modern Iranian history is emblematic of this interpretive elasticity that discourses of Islam afford their followers. Islam in Iran (and elsewhere) is an invention of the mind.[4]

---

[2] I have expressed this on the eve of the thirty-sixth anniversary of the revolution in an interview with *Tehran Times*, 'Iranians rose against Shah to gain freedom', 10 February 2015. Available at www.tehrantimes.com/component/content/article/93-interviews/121728-iranians-rose-against-shah-to-gain-freedom-justice-scholar (accessed 11 March 2015).

[3] See further Arshin Adib-Moghaddam, 'Global intifadah? September 11th and the Struggle within Islam', *Cambridge Review of International Affairs*, Vol. 15, No. 2 (2002), pp. 203–16.

[4] For a recent examination of the dialectic between Islam and liberalism see Joseph Massad, *Islam in Liberalism*, Chicago: University of Chicago Press, 2015. For Western

A few historical examples will illustrate what I mean by such elasticity. It is generally agreed that the first modern mass upheaval in Iranian history occurred in 1891, when Ayatollah Mirza Hossein Shirazi issued a *fatwa* (religious opinion) forbidding his followers to use any tobacco-based products. He did this in response to the concession of exclusive tobacco rights in favour of Major G. Talbot, a British citizen who endeavoured to establish the Imperial Tobacco Company in Persia, which Iranians saw as a Trojan horse for further British imperial control of the country. A *fatwa* by a *marja-ye taghlid* (source of emulation) has an important impact on pious Shias comparable to an edict by the Pope for believing Catholics. Hence the repercussions were immediate.

The role of Ayatollah Shirazi was certainly important, and his activism is analytically pertinent given that it galvanised the clerical strata into a politically active role. Nevertheless, several strata of Iranian society expressed opposition to the Qajar monarchy at the end of the nineteenth century. The revolt was aided and abetted by a range of individuals and movements. The role of Jamaladin al-Afghani (also known as Asadabadi), one of the most prolific and prominent non-clerical pan-Islamists, for instance, has not been sufficiently explored in the scholarly literature.[5] Yet it was al-Afghani who colluded with leading clerics in the seminaries of Qom and Najaf to galvanise protests against the tobacco concession. This explains the transcendental power of the movement, i.e., it moved beyond and motivated several strata of society. As a result of this resistance to the Qajar monarchy, al-Afghani was exiled to Iraq, from where he continued to agitate against the concession and Iran's dependence on foreign powers. The ensuing revolts, which started in Shiraz and

---

misperceptions see also the introduction to Arshin Adib-Moghaddam, *On the Arab Revolts and the Iranian Revolution*.

[5] For a recent exception see Umar Ryad, 'Anti-imperialism and the Pan-Islamic Movement', in David Motadel, *Islam and the European Empires*, Oxford: Oxford University Press, 2014, pp. 131–49.

moved to Tabriz and from there to Isfahan and elsewhere, prompted Nasseredin Shah to revoke the concession.

With the Tobacco revolts, we find for the first time in modern Iranian history, a mass upheaval with transversal potentiality against the monarchy and in opposition to outside interference in Iranian affairs. With al-Afghani, and later on with his Egyptian disciple Muhammad Abduh, an Islam emerged that was geared towards themes such as progress and independence. Freedom was not sought merely from oppressive governments but also from imperialism, in this case in its British variant. Subsequently, Al-Afghani was also a great proponent of the constitutional revolt in Iran, which occurred primarily between 1906 and 7. This upheaval led to the establishment of a constitutional monarchy in Iran and entrenched the vocabulary of liberalism and republicanism in the country. As with the tobacco revolt, freedom was not associated merely with opposition to the Qajar monarchs but also with being against imperialism. After all, during this period, Britain and Russia agreed to divide Iran into 'spheres of influence': the north was designated a zone of exclusive Russian influence, the south a zone of exclusive British influence and the centre of the county, including the capital, Tehran, was designated as a neutral zone. This agreement was an imperial response to Iran establishing a parliament and adopting the country's first modern constitution in 1906. Iran's experiment with constitutional monarchy lasted until 1921, when Reza Khan took over the state in a coup d'état and eventually established the authoritarian Pahlavi monarchy. The British and Russians (as the Soviet Union) jointly intervened in 1941, this time to oust Reza Shah. Thereafter, Britain would remain the dominant external force in Iranian affairs at least until 1971, when British forces retreated from the Persian Gulf.

The third example, and perhaps the most consequential for the Islamic revolution in 1979, was the nationalisation of Iran's oil company under the premiership of Dr. Mohammad Mossadegh between 1951 and 3. Dr. Mossadegh was Iran's first democratically elected Prime Minister. When he came to power in 1951, he nationalised the

Anglo Iranian Oil Company (out of which British Petroleum emerged) and endeavoured to establish a viable democratic order in Iran. In 1953, he was ousted by a CIA/MI6 engineered coup d'état, which re-established the dictatorship of Mohammad Reza Pahlavi, who subsequently ruled the country as a key Western ally until the Islamic revolution in 1979, as discussed above. In all the examples of modern mass movements in Iran we find a recurring dialectic: opposition to psycho-nationalism on the one side and opposition to external interference in Iranian affairs on the other. Ultimately, the aim was a freer society, a pluralistic order in terms of governance and independence from external powers. Narratives employing Islamic imagery, symbols and norms repeatedly were used in order to accentuate this quest for a freer polity in Iran. Even nationalists such as Mossadegh had a progressive vision of the role of Islam in Iranian politics. He would have agreed that Islam is not inherently anti-democratic and illiberal, which may explain why figureheads of his National Front coalition, such as Mehdi Bazargan, later believed in the Islamic revolution. I will discuss their vision of an 'Islamic-democratic' republic in Iran in the following section.

OF GOVERNANCE AND LIBERTY

The two grand ambitions of Iran's modern history, democracy and independence, were central to the Islamic revolution as well. The mainstream of the Iranian revolutionaries imagined an authentic Iranian-Islamic order that would be accountable to the people and independent of the dictates of external powers. It was the culmination of the protest of Iranians against both their political masters and the international system enveloping their country, as expressed in their revolutionary slogans, *nasharghi nagharbi jomhuri-ye islami* (neither east nor west, only the Islamic republic) and *esteghlal, azadi jomhuri-ye islami* (independence, freedom, Islamic republic). Iran, even today, is in many ways trying to bridge the tensions between these slogans. Even Khomeini had to engage with these narratives in order to boost his position within the revolutionary struggle.

OF GOVERNANCE AND LIBERTY 131

If freedom and democracy were not at the heart of the demands of the revolutionaries, Khomeini would not have been forced to refer to the 'God-given right of freedom and liberty' that Islam guarantees and to accentuate that 'freedom is the primary right of humans' at the beginning of the revolution, promises he breached rather blatantly once his vision for the Iranian state was institutionalised.[6] Khomeini spoke liberal and acted authoritarian, not least because he was more concerned with solidifying the power of the state than the sovereignty of the people. In this sense, Khomeini was typically modernist – a state builder par excellence because he understood that any modern state needs a sophisticated and multilayered bureaucracy and institutional framework to claim and exert its sovereignty both vis-à-vis the people and the international system.[7] Psycho-nationalism mind games were central to this process.

Mehdi Bazargan provides an interesting example of how an Islam was invented in the build up to the Iranian revolution, was amenable to democracy and a liberal order within society, and stood in opposition to a totalitarian interpretation of the state. Bazargan had been the first director of the National Iranian Oil Company (NIOC) after its nationalisation during the Mossadegh premiership. In 1961, he founded the Freedom Movement of Iran, which included such iconoclastic figures of Iran's intellectual and political scene as Ayatollah Mahmoud Taleqani, Ali Shariati and Yadollah Sahabi. In 1977, he inaugurated the Human Rights Association of Iran. For this generation of Iran's political class, Islam was a conduit to institute pluralism, human rights and democracy. In this vein, the charter of the Freedom Movement of Iran declares that the 'servitude of God requires refusal of servitude to any other master. Gratefulness to God is contingent upon gaining freedom and utilising it to attain rights,

---

[6] Mohammad-Hossein Jamshidi (ed.), *Andisheh-e siasi-ye Imam Khomeini* [Political Thought of Imam Khomeini], Tehran: Pajoheshkade-ye Imam Khomeini va enghelab-islami, 1384 [2005], pp. 245, 246, my translation.
[7] See further Arshin Adib-Moghaddam (ed.), *A Critical Introduction to Khomeini*, Cambridge: Cambridge University Press, 2014.

justice, and service.'[8] For Bazargan himself, 'freedom is God's gift to His steward on earth, humankind. Whoever takes away this freedom is guilty of the greatest treason against humankind.'[9] Obviously, Bazargan was opposed to the absolutist interpretation of Islam that the Khomeinist forces espoused in their emphasis on the total sovereignty of the Supreme Jurisprudent (*velayat-e faqi-ye motlaq*), who would be positioned at the helm of the state. 'Islamic government', Bazargan argued 'cannot help but be at once consultative, democratic, and divinely inspired.'[10] It must follow from this that 'in Islamic government the relations among individuals and the administration of society are predicated upon relative shared freedom and mutual responsibility'. In more concrete terms this means that 'Islam permits difference of opinions even within the realm of the tenets of religion, let alone in administrative and governmental issues. Shia theology under the rubric of *ijtihad* [independent reasoning]', Bazargan pointed out, 'has left the gate of such debates open until the end of the time and the coming of the messiah.'[11]

Consequently, the Supreme Jurisprudent or any 'source of imitation' (the highest Shia authority) cannot claim to be infallible. Citizens should be free to express their grievances because 'freedom means the freedom to oppose, criticize, and object – even if the criticism is untrue and unjust. Where there is freedom there are opponents and currents that disturb routine stability and normalcy.'[12] In terms of governance all of this translates into the 'principle of division of powers and their mutual non-interference and orderly checks and balances'. The Islamic corpus, the Quran and the *sunna* [Prophet's practices], according to this interpretation of Bazargan, is intrinsically just and partial to freedom of choice: 'God bestows both

---

[8] Mehdi Bazargan, 'Religion and Liberty', in Charles Kurzman (ed.), *Liberal Islam: A Sourcebook*, Oxford: Oxford University Press, 1998, p. 77.
[9] Ibid.
[10] Ibid., p. 79.
[11] Ibid.
[12] Ibid., p. 81.

freedom and guidance concerning the consequences of actions. His mercy is infinite and His vengeance great.' In the end, individuals must choose for themselves: 'Freedom exists, so do responsibility and restraint. The choice is ours.'[13]

Ayatollah Taleqani, perhaps the most prominent clerical ally of Bazargan, shared this emphasis on freedom and individual choice. Ayatollah Taleqani was one of the co-founders of the Freedom Movement of Iran. His discourse typically blended leftist ideas into his vision of Islam. Prominent among the Iranian intelligentsia and opposed to Khomeini's doctrine of the *velayat-e faqih* (rule of the Supreme Jurisprudent), Taleqani argued that 'government must be like the representative and deputy of individuals and not the representative of a special class ... Its purpose is nothing but the preservation of individual rights and of the collectivity of individuals.'[14] It must follow that 'government does not have the right to deprive or limit the freedom and independence of individuals or the rights of some classes for the profit of another class in the name of the higher good of the government'.[15] In the last sermon Taleqani delivered before his death in September 1979, in a period when his opposition to Khomeini became more explicit, he emphasised that the goal of the Prophet Mohammad himself was to 'free the people, to free them from class oppression, to free them from pagan thoughts which had been imposed upon them, to free them from the ordinances and laws which [were] imposed for the benefit of one group, one class, over others'.[16] According to Taleqani, the 'call of Islam is the call to mercy and freedom'. With reference to the Quran he accentuated that 'even the sinner who is condemned to death – under Islamic law there is mercy for him too ... His [the prophet's] *jihad* [religious struggle]

---

[13] Ibid., p. 84.
[14] Ayatollah Mahmud Taleqani, 'The Characteristics of Islamic Economics', in John J. Donohue and John L. Esposito (eds.), *Islam in Transition: Muslim Perspectives*, Oxford: Oxford University Press, 2007, p. 233.
[15] Ibid.
[16] Mahmud Taleqani, 'Taleqani's Last Sermon', in Kurzman (ed.), *Liberal Islam*, p. 47.

was mercy, his *hijra* [migration from Mecca to Medina] was mercy, his laws were mercy, his guidance over principles was mercy – the Islamic order ought to be based on mercy.'[17]

The revolutionary reality on the ground bitterly disappointed these lofty views, couched in notions of freedom of expression, democratic Islamic governance and human rights. The anarchic environment of Iran did not lend itself to the calm and collected paradigm put forward by Taleqani, Bazargan and others. The daily battles for power and the frantic, utopian hope for a better future for Iranians after the departure of the shah in January 1979, gave impetus to revolutionary radicalism and the politics of antagonism that Bazargan and his allies tried to minimise.[18] The reality was that Bazargan and his cabinet were increasingly powerless and that the Revolutionary Council dominated by hardliners held the real power. In March 1979, Bazargan submitted his resignation, but Khomeini rejected his request, not least in order to stabilise the state. A month later, amidst increasing revolutionary chaos in Iran, Bazargan and the members of his cabinet escaped an assassination attempt. Frustrated over the hostage takeover at the US embassy, Bazargan and his cabinet finally resigned in November 1979. In November 1982, he expressed his criticism about the situation in Iran to the then speaker of parliament, Ali-Akbar Rafsanjani:

> The government has created an atmosphere of terror, fear, revenge and national disintegration . . . What has the ruling elite done in nearly four years, besides bringing death and destruction, packing the prisons and the cemeteries in every city, creating long queues, shortages, high prices, unemployment, poverty, homeless people, repetitious slogans and a dark future?[19]

---

[17] Ibid.
[18] For the impact on the region see Adib-Moghaddam, *The International Politics of the Persian Gulf*.
[19] 'Khomeini's Grip Appears at Its Tightest', *The New York Times*, 21 November 1982.

Bazargan died in 1995, yet the idea that Islam could foster a liberal order continued to be put forward by a range of intellectuals, politicians and reformist clerics. The dual ambition of Iranian contemporary history – to gain independence from foreign dictates and to democratise governance in the country – continues to be expressed to this day.[20]

REFORMED REVOLUTIONARIES

The psycho-nationalist momentum of 1979 established a central political dynamic in Iran: intellectuals and leaders who were too 'loudly' pro-reformist and too overtly in favour of democracy were silenced, incarcerated, purged or exiled. Mehdi Bazargan and Ayatollah Taleqani were among the lucky ones. They escaped assassination attempts and remained in their country without being incarcerated. The 'second' wave of reformists opposed to the authoritarian, post-revolutionary order in Iran was less fortunate. Liberal Islamic thinkers such as Abdolkarim Soroush, Mohsen Kadivar and Hasan Eshkevari have been forced into exile without recourse to any institutional resources in Iran. The trajectory of the fate of Soroush is emblematic of these devoured children of the revolution. Soroush was a member of the Cultural Revolution Council, which was responsible for reforming the universities in accordance with new revolutionary realities (education being a typical target of psycho-nationalism, as discussed throughout this study). In retrospect, he has tried to downplay the role of the Council in the purges of scholars, in particular in the Humanities and Social Sciences, and the closure of the universities to those ends. According to him, the 'purges did not start in universities at any rate, nor were they initiated or continued in universities by the Cultural Revolution Institute'.[21] Yet at the same time he concedes that 'the first things that happened on the morrow

---

[20] For recent views on the spectre of dissidence in Iran see Lucian Stone (ed.), *Iranian Identity and Cosmopolitanism: Spheres of Belonging*, New York: Bloomsbury, 2014.
[21] Abdolkarim Soroush, 'Sense and Nonsense: About the Cultural Revolution Again'. Available at www.drsoroush.com/English/By_DrSoroush/sense&nonsense.html (accessed 11 February 2015).

of the victory of the revolution [were] purges.' These were not decreed by the Cultural Revolution Institute of which he was a member, he claims, but primarily political in nature. 'Most of the political groups supported them,' Soroush maintains,

> it was only the Prime Minister [Bazargan] of the provisional government who objected . . . And he managed, within the limits of his powers, to reduce the number of purges, although, of course, this earned him some curses from those clerics and political activists who didn't like him and who called him a colluder. As to the expulsion of academics, if the Revolution Council asked the University of Tehran's chancellor to participate in the purges and to expel professors – and he assented – it never put such a request, even implicitly, to the Cultural Revolution Institute and there was no suggestion of it in Imam Khomeini's letter to the institute either.[22]

Soroush clearly is trying to address the allegations that he was part of the problem and that his calls for reforms today are hypocritical. Certainly he was not known for opposing the purges when he was a member of the Cultural Revolution Council. At the same time he was a small cog in a big revolutionary machine and was simply not in a position to decide the fate of others. The legacy of Soroush likely will not be determined by his role during the revolution; rather his writings about democracy and secularism are likely to continue to appeal to future generations of Iranians, especially those with a religious background.

The writing of Soroush is heavily laden with complex, philosophical concepts that are used in order to put forward an interpretive, hermeneutical approach to the corpus of Islam, i.e., the Quran, the *sunnah* and the *hadiths*. From his perspective, knowledge about Islam expands and contracts with reference to historical circumstances: 'The theory of the contraction and expansion of religious interpretation', Soroush claims, 'separates religion and religious knowledge, considers

[22] Ibid.

the latter as a branch of human knowledge, and regards our understanding of religion as evolving along with other branches of human knowledge.'[23] This distinction merits and requires constant reform and renewal through *ijtihad* [independent reasoning]. 'To treat religious knowledge, a branch of human knowledge, as incomplete, impure, insufficient, and culture-bound; to try to mend and darn its wears and tears is, in itself, an admirable and hallowed undertaking.'[24] Given that religious knowledge never really can be complete, it cannot be monopolised by one religious leader. 'The acceptance of the sovereignty of religion is far from putting one's own words in the Prophet's mouth and arrogating his seat to oneself.' Rather the contrary. For Soroush, it 'means a sincere attempt to understand his message through repeated consultation with the sacred text and the tradition. Scholars of religion have no other status or service than this.'[25]

Comparable to Bazargan and Taleqani, Soroush calls for a pluralistic understanding of Islam and a democratic order based on spiritual values. Within such an 'Islamic-democratic' polity, human rights would have to be cultivated and secured, given that 'a religion that is oblivious to human rights (including the need of humanity for freedom and justice) is not tenable in the modern world. In other words, religion needs to be right not only logically but also ethically.'[26] Soroush does not explicitly address the plight of non-believers within such a religiously inspired system, but in his writings and lectures he repeatedly alludes to the freedom of choice that any Islamic government must ensure:

> To be sure, contemporary advocates of human rights can claim no monopoly on truth and justice; nevertheless, religious societies, precisely because of their religious nature, need to seriously engage

---

[23] Abdolkarim Soroush, 'Islamic Revival and Reform: Theological Approaches', in Mahmoud Sadri and Ahmad Sadri (eds., trans.), *Reason, Freedom and Democracy in Islam: Essential Writings of Abdolkarim Soroush*, Oxford: Oxford University Press, 2000, p. 33.
[24] Ibid., p. 32.
[25] Ibid., p. 37.
[26] Abdolkarim Souroush, 'The Idea of Democratic Religious Government', in Sadri and Sadri (eds., trans.), *Reason, Freedom and Democracy*, p. 128.

> in discussion of the issues they pose. Not only did our predecessors passionately debate such extrareligious issues as the question of free choice and the question of the limits of God's rights to overburden the faithful with religious obligations, but Islamic society felt a religious obligation to allow such debates to spread and prosper. By the same token, the extrareligious debates of our day, which happen to concern human rights, must be viewed as worthy and useful exchanges of opinions in Islamic society. The partisans in these debates deserve a blessed respect, and the outcome of such discussions should be heeded and implemented by the governments . . . Observing human rights (such as justice, freedom, and so on) guarantees not only the democratic character of a government, but also its religious character.[27]

As indicated, Soroush is rather abstract, metaphysical, almost gnostic in his writings and lectures. Mohsen Kadivar, who emerged as one of the most influential reformist clerics in Iran, until he was harassed into exile in the United States in 2008, addresses the themes of democracy and liberalism, including the rights of non-believers, in rather more explicit terms, quite comparable to the affirmation of freedom and democracy by Bazargan and Ayatollah Taleqani. In this vein, Kadivar suggests that 'freedom of religion and belief means an individual's right to freely choose any and all ideologies and religions he likes'.[28] In addition, this refers to the 'freedom and the right to think, to have beliefs and values, to express one's religion and opinions, to partake in religious rites and practices . . . and to be able to freely critique one's religion'.[29] According to Kadivar, even non-believers (*kuffar*) should not be punished for their beliefs: 'The persecution of a heathen is unjustified in Islam. Through renewed *ijtihad* (independent reasoning) and based on the correct principles of the Quran and

---

[27] Ibid., p. 129.
[28] Mohsen Kadivar, 'Freedom of Religion and Belief in Islam', in Mehran Kamrava (ed.), *The New Voices of Islam: Reforming Politics and Modernity*, London: I.B. Tauris, 2006, p. 119.
[29] Ibid., pp. 119–20.

the *hadith*, freedom of religion and belief can be achieved through Islam.'[30] Comparable to Bazargan, who refers to God-given parameters framing a free society,[31] Kadivar indicates that Islam represents 'the correct and just religion' and warns of 'divine punishment at the end of time',[32] but he maintains that Islam secures the 'right of choice in beliefs and in actions in all areas so long as these beliefs and actions do not deprive others of their rights or do not disturb public peace and order'. While it is legitimate and salutary to invite others to embrace Islam (*dawa*), Kadivar reiterates that the Quran explicitly states that there is no compulsion in religion. It must follow quite rationally that,

> non-Muslims living inside or outside Muslim lands have peace and security so long as they do not wage war on Islam. Whether or not they believe in one of the sanctioned religions or in falsehood, no Muslim has the right to disrupt their peace simply because their beliefs are different. This assertion is substantiated by the eternally valid verses of the Quran ... To sum up, even though most of the interpretations of Islam that are prevalent today augur poorly for freedom of religion and belief, a more correct interpretation, based on the sacred text and valid traditions, finds Islam highly supportive of freedom of thought and religion and easily in accord with the principles of human rights.[33]

WAYS FORWARD: THE QUESTION OF ISLAMIC SECULARISM

A common thread is apparent here. The set of thinkers covered in this chapter reinvent an Islam as a *via media* between the authoritarian status quo in Iran (and the Arab world) and a liberal order that would ensure democracy, freedom of belief and religion and ultimately a liberated society. I have conceptualised this as psycho-therapeutic

---

[30] Ibid., p. 120.
[31] Bazargan, 'Religion and Liberty', in Kurzman (ed.), *Liberal Islam*, p. 83.
[32] Kadivar, 'Freedom of Religion', p. 120.
[33] Kadivar, 'Freedom of Religion', p. 142.

resistance acting upon psycho-nationalist power. Islam is reconceptualised as inherently pluralistic, just, accommodating, non-doctrinal and essentially democratic. Islam is mercy, Taleqani argued. Islam demands human rights, Soroush suggests. Islam means freedom, Bazargan maintained. Islam liberates the mind, Kadivar accentuates. Equally, Hasan Eshkevari, another staunch supporter of the Iranian reform movement, is convinced that Islam 'regardless of how it may be interpreted, cannot endorse the killing of innocent people under any circumstances. There is no Islamic text that backs up such an action.'[34]

In all these theories of Islam, freedom comes first and religious ordinances are relegated to individual choice. Islam, in this hermeneutical re-evaluation, essentially is secularised. At the same time, even this secular Islam retains its identitarian precepts and an underlying sense of superiority. While accentuating the role of Islam in liberating and democratising society, there continues to be a hierarchy, at the top of which we find the enlightened Muslim who speaks in an Iranian-Shia accent with European undertones. Islam, now cleansed from authoritarianism and re-imagined as the reincarnation of liberty, continues to be prioritised and idealised. Despite his emphasis on freedom of choice, Kadivar maintains that Islam is the 'correct and just religion', that there are 'false religious and doctrinal beliefs' and that the Quran warns 'those who turn their back on the Just Religion of divine punishment at the end of time'.[35] Soroush shares a similar conviction in the superiority and necessity of an Islamic order when he implies that 'democratic religious regimes need not wash their hands of religiosity nor turn their backs on God's approval'.[36] The approval of God continues to be central and 'entails religious awareness that is leavened by a more authentic and humane understanding of religiosity and that endeavours to guide the people in accordance with these ideals'.[37] In

[34] Hasan Yousefi Eshkevari, 'God's Uprooted Warriors'. Available at http://yousefieshkevari.com/?p=2103 (accessed 12 January 2015).
[35] Kadivar, 'Freedom of Religion', *The New Voices*, p. 120.
[36] Soroush, *Reason, Freedom and Democracy*, p. 128.
[37] Ibid.

this view, the non-religious rest continues to be pasted into a religious core defined by guiding authorities. Bazargan is equally ambiguous when he says that 'God has given us freedom of opinion and action within certain parameters, but He has given us plenty of warning . . . that rebellion, *disbelief*, and injustice will have dire results . . . both in this life and in the hereafter.'[38] The object continues to be Allah and the right path continues to be signposted by the *surahs* of the Quran (and the *hadiths*): 'God bestows both freedom and guidance concerning the consequences of actions. His mercy is infinite and His vengeance great.'[39] For all these believers there seems to be a correct world view, the right choice, an ideal order. It is implicit that it should be Islamic and there is even a rather arrogant expectation that in the end it will be.

The problem seems to be that these proclamations are made in the name of Islam, not humanity. There remains then a problematic, almost patronising aftertaste even in what I have called 'secular Islam', exactly because lofty ideals such as freedom and democracy are claimed to be the purview of one religious community. There is not enough syntactical and narrative emphasis on the universality of these norms and the global struggles that brought them about. In essence we are all humans (*bashar*), as Shariati pointed out before the revolution in his opposition against the shah. Becoming human (*insan*) is a universal project shared by *humankind*, which is why Shariati's prose repeatedly is littered with references to Nietzsche, Sartre, Buddha, Iqbal or the Indian philosopher (and statesman) Sarvepalli Radhakishnan (1888–1975), and why he stresses that it is science that can help *humankind* 'to completely free themselves'.[40] Compared to the cosmopolitan style of Shariati, the narratives of the secular Islamists covered in this article seem rather provincial, despite nods to Popper, Rumi and others. At base, secular Islam remains an identitarian project that does not sufficiently connect

---

[38] Bazargan, 'Religion and Liberty', in Kurzman (ed.), *Liberal Islam*, p. 83, emphasis added.
[39] Ibid., p. 84.
[40] Ali Shariati, 'Humanity and Islam', in Kurzman (ed.), *Liberal Islam*, p. 193.

the Muslim 'self' to the rest of humanity. Bahais, Christians, Jews, Heathens, Hindus, Buddhists, Zoroastrians, homosexuals, etc., continue to linger on the side roads of the Islamic highway. In such an idealised Islamic democratic order, judicial equality could be ensured, but true cultural egalitarianism remains confined. Muslims continue to be imagined at the top of a hierarchy that differentiates between human beings on the basis of their religious convictions. In order to refine the secular Islamic viewpoint, it would have to start with a universal understanding of history, and to be represented from the perspective of minorities within the Islamic realm.

Why is it that Islam has to appear with such vehement force in the first place? The term appears at every twist and turn of the narratives covered in this article. It is almost obsessive, certainly syntactically repetitive and even redundant. Obviously, it has a lot to do with context. Iran is an Islamic Republic and there exists an authoritarian state that rules in the name of Islam. All of the thinkers covered in my analysis are at odds with the state, so they have to address and challenge its 'Islamicity'. Exactly because of this, however, a central paradox ensues: in order to reinvent a liberal Islam that could do battle with a doctrinaire one, Islam has to be stretched so widely that it remains rather heavy with religion, even after its secular diet. When Glasnost met orthodox Soviet communism, it was still sold as Leninist ideology by Gorbachev. Comparably, secular Islam continues to confine itself within the original revolutionary project, for instance by reimagining Khomeini as a reformer or Mohammad as a democrat. It is preaching to the converted, but its syntax does not appeal to the non-believer who wasn't part of the Islamic universe in the first place.

In this sense, secular Islam lags behind the thought of classical Muslim philosophers, in particular Ibn Sina (Avicenna), who appears as a reference point in the writings of Soroush and Kadivar but remains insufficiently conceptualised. Indeed, in the writings of these philosophers, the notion of a superior Islamic way is almost entirely absent. Islam emerges as an *a priori*, an entirely abstract nodal point that was yet to be conquered intellectually. We therefore must distinguish between this 'a priori Islam' of the classical philosophers and the rather more 'concrete Islam' of the so-called 'Islamic revivalists' from the nineteenth century onwards. *A priori* Islam disperses with political utilitarianism and the politics of identity, it cannot afford a fundamentalist or literalist reading of the Quran, it is not ideological and it does not Islamise reality. It does not refer to a multiplicity of syntheses, every one of which constitutes an individual discourse articulated towards some concrete notion of Islam's meaning. Islam is there, a desired object, yet it is *a priori* to our existence, it is not a concrete definition of a place into which we easily can venture. (Islamic ontology, the Islam we think we can see, is not that of a totality, but rather that of an engineered totalisation that changes in accordance with the determinations of history and time. Thus, the ontology of any Islamic field must be entirely dependent on the process of human construction.) The classical philosophers were central to illuminating this *a priori* existence of Islam that does not yield a significant boundary between self and other. In their writings the ontology of Islam is stretched so thin, resembling an infinite horizontal line, that the points of contact with adjacent discursivities are exponentially multiplied. Their ideas are the true antithesis to the bio-politics of identity.

For instance, in Ibn Sina's seminal *danish-namaha-yealai* (Treatise on Knowledge), philosophy takes on a forward-looking modality. In his *uyun al-hikmah*, Ibn Sina writes that *al-hikmah* (which he uses to mean the same as philosophy) 'is the perfection of the human soul through conceptualisation [*tasawwur*] of things and judgment [*tasdiq*] of theoretical and practical realities to the measure of human ability'.[41] He went on in his later writings to distinguish between Peripatetic philosophy and what he called 'Oriental philosophy' (*al-hikmat al-mashriqi'yah*) which was not based on ratiocination alone, but included revealed knowledge (it also set the stage for the influential treatises of Sohravardi, and here especially his *kitab hikmat al-ishraq*). There is a particularly striking poem by Ibn Sina about the fate of the human soul (note it is not exclusive to Muslims),

---

[41] Ibn Sina, *Fontessapientiae (uyun al-hikmah)*, edited by Abdurrahman Badawied, Cairo: no publisher, 1954, p. 16.

which exemplifies this emphasis on congruence between rational analysis and spiritual opportunity that was central to the canons of the classical philosophers of Islam.

> Until when the hour of its homeward flight draws near,
> And 'tis time for it to return to its ampler sphere,
> It carols with joy, for the veil is raised, and it spies
> Such things as cannot be witnessed by waking eyes.
> On a lofty height doth it warble its songs of praise
> (for even the lowliest being doth knowledge raise).
> And so it returneth, aware of all hidden things
> In the universe, while no stain to its garment clings.[42]

The ultimate object here is the perfection of the intellectual faculties of the individual, who does not carry an exclusive identity, who is only presumed in his or her physical constitution. There is no realm of knowledge that is exclusive to Muslims in the writings of Ibn Sina, no discernible schematic dichotomy that permeates his narratives. He searches for a supreme truth, not a supreme civilisation or race. He and many of his contemporaries managed to create the archives of classical philosophy without the emergence of a discourse that would legitimate subjugation of the other, without a call to arms and without proclamations of righteousness. Yet, the Islamic secularists that I have covered above share with their ideological, Islamist counterparts the conviction of superiority despite the nascent philosophical and critical content of their ideas. They continue to adhere to the viewpoint that Muslims hold the holy grail of truth and that they are obliged to invite and persuade others to understand it. This is certainly not their ambition, but Islam, even in this liberal garb, easily could be turned into another form of hegemony. In such a dystopian world, war and aggression would not be justified in terms of killing the infidels but of civilising them.

---

[42] Quoted in Richard Walzer, *Greek into Arabic: Essays on Islamic Philosophy*, Cambridge, MA: Harvard University Press, 1962, p. 26.

6 Sexing the Nation: Subversive Trans-localities

This chapter presents a final assessment of the preceding analysis with particular emphasis on the 'national question' asked at the beginning of the study. I have argued in this book that national narratives are never immutable; they are impure, creolised phenomena, porous and polluted spaces that are open to interpretive manipulation. In order to govern that reality, psycho-nationalisms are socially engineered to simulate uniformity and positive distinction from the 'other'. In this sense, psycho-nationalism is a border creating device, it is meant to create 'iron walls' staffed by intolerant gatekeepers. In its traditional manifestation it provokes distinctly fascist politics. In apartheid South Africa and in Israel among the right wing, it has informed policies of separation and oppression. And in continental Europe today, it is challenging the idea of the European Union in the name of an anti-immigration agenda – borders are re-staffed, barbwires rolled out and fences are being put up. The resurgence of the politics of identity spearheaded by Geert Wilders and Marine Le Pen is a strong contemporary indicator of the dangers of psycho-nationalism. The so-called 'Left' is trapped in ideological controversy that merely proclaims a counter-identity, admittedly more optimistic, but without a great leap towards a politics of radical federal democracy that empowers citizens and communities rather than the central state.

And yet in my previous book I have shown that any effort to separate the 'self' from the 'other' creates a very particular form of interdependence, a 'disjunctive synthesis' that does not yield neatly delineated identities. Thus, representations of 'self' and 'other' are entirely interdependent even when they are geared towards antagonistic politics. The preceding chapters gave empirical support to that claim. Iranians may have parodied seemingly divergent identities with their significant others – Arabs, Europeans, Americans – aimed at setting themselves apart as a separate and authentic 'nation', but their performative acts achieved the opposite. By allocating to the other side a prominent discursive presence, the interdependence between the national narratives suggesting 'an Iran' are now entirely dependent on the ideational territory presumed to be beyond those imagined confines. In other words, Iran's significant 'others' are now entirely subsumed in the meaning of Iran. This is reflected in the writings of the new, post-Islamist intellectuals of the country, as demonstrated in the last chapter, whose ideas reveal this expanded meaning of Iran which appears in dialogue rather than in opposition to the 'other'. Moreover, this creolised space is lived on a daily basis in Iran itself, and more explicitly by the millions of Iranians outside of the country. As one of my interviewees in Hamburg said: 'I have never been to Iran, but even as a German, I feel that I am incomplete without my Persian heritage... Eid-e Nowrouz continues to be the most celebrated party in our household.'[1] In other words: meanings of Iran continue to be lived and celebrated on a daily basis beyond the confines of the nation-state and its purveyors.

It is not only that the meaning of Iran is co-produced quite explicitly by 'exiles'; as an idea and historical reality Iran is scattered around the world. Manifestations of Persia even stare you in the face in the Buddhist temples of Japan. For instance in the gorgeous Sanjusangen-do temple in Kyoto built in 1164, where one of the famous 1,000 life size statues represents Ahura Mazda, the Zoroastrian god whose depiction entered the temple as an important deity via India and China. There are thousands of additional such examples that connect Iran to the world and global history to Iran. Similar world narratives can be written for other so-called 'nations' if they are liberated from the confines of psycho-nationalism.

There is a second, even more straightforward reason why 'self' and 'other' can never really be detached. At base, our biological

[1] Cyrus E., Interview, Berlin, 28 December 2016.

constitution as human beings is our primordial 'identity' which is shared beyond religious affiliations and nationalisms. As Ali Shariati said in a lecture given during the emerging revolutionary atmosphere of late 1960s Iran: there are two meanings to being human. '*Bashar*', he explains, 'is that particular being that contains physiological characteristics which are shared by all humans.'[2] Let's call him Donald Trump. *Insan*, on the other side, has a rather more normative connotation. Let's call him Jesus. 'Bashar is a "being" while insan is a "becoming."'[3] To become *insan* we have to foster three traits: our self-consciousness, our ability to make choices and our ability to create things. The aim of humanity is to attain the highest form of consciousness, to become *insan*. But mind you, Shariati warns, 'becoming *insan* is not a stationary event, rather, it is a perpetual process of becoming and an everlasting evolution towards infinity'.[4] From Trump to Jesus: this is the journey from mere existence as a human being to loving your neighbour. So in this way, *insaniyat* becomes a process of becoming. Shariati stresses that we should not think of *insaniyat* as a destination, but as a never-ending journey. 'Thus, from among all humans, everyone is as much *bashar* as the rest, but there are some who *have attained insanyat*, and there are others who are *in the process of becoming* an *insan*, either little or to an exalting degree.'[5] The emergence of a humane consciousness which is characteristic of attaining *insaniyat*, must always be precipitated, even constituted by some kind of force, which is why Shariati focuses on the human tendency to revolt against injustice, a theme that he explores in close relation to the killing of Hussein at the battle of Kerbala in 680 AD, the martyrdom of Jesus and other religious figures.

---

[2] Ali Shariati, 'Humanity and Islam', in Charles Kuzman (ed.), *Liberal Islam: A Sourcebook*, Oxford: Oxford University Press, 1998, p. 188.
[3] Ibid.
[4] Ibid., p. 189.
[5] Ibid., p. 188, emphasis added. See further Arshin Adib-Moghaddam, 'Remnants of Empire: Civilisation, Torture and Racism in the War on Terrorism', in Michael Patrick Cullinane and David Ryan (eds.), *U.S. Foreign Policy and the Other*, New York: Berghahn, 2014, pp. 222–34.

For Shariati, it is precisely these monumental epics of human history that function as the signifiers of justice vs. injustice.

Such humanistic philosophy has a long tradition in the non-western world. Indeed, Columbia University professor Hamid Dabashi has recently sketched a map of literary humanism in Persia that dates back over 1,400 years.[6] In Iran and elsewhere, life-affirming practices from 'below' such as philosophy, art and poetry have repeatedly intervened in the state-sanctioned making of psycho-nationalism (Islamo-centric or nationalistic). Furthermore, other scholarship has demonstrated that there is a long tradition of 'feminist' thinking in Iran which has recurrently eroded the 'phallocentric' writing of Iranian history and the de-feminised identity discourse contained therein. Iranian feminists have long decried the 'masculinity' of Iranian history and the patriarchal interpretation of the Islamic canon, including sharia law.[7] The activism and scholarship of Iranian women has dislocated the testosterone-ridden meaning of Iran, exactly because Iranian psycho-nationalism has claimed the whole individual, attempting to transcend his/her identity as a sexual being. There is an opportunity at this historical juncture, a period with residual post-national hope, to reflect on the functions of women for the ideological constitution of the state and the nation.

If national narratives are characterised by their 'in-between-ness' within global structures, as I have claimed, if the true meaning of Iran transcends its historical narration, then there should be an equally interesting shift in the gendered discourse about the country towards, perhaps, a 'trans-sexual' understanding of Iranian-ness, that is neither entirely male, nor female. Such future research probes the possibilities of this transsexual constitution of the national subject in Iran as an exercise in negating the patriarchal masculinity of Iranian

---

[6] See further Hamid Dabashi, *Persian Literary Humanism*.
[7] Ziba Mir-Hosseini has written about this among others. See her *Islam and Gender: The Religious Debate in Contemporary Iran*, London: I.B. Tauris, 2000.

psycho-nationalism.[8] The female body, after all, has been a battle ground in modern Iranian history in typically psycho-nationalist fashion. From the ban of veiling announced by Reza Shah in 1936, which was inspired by the secular doctrines of Kemalism in Turkey, the enforced veiling after the revolution and prohibitions of women to enter 'contentious' public spaces such as football stadiums, to internet campaigns where men veil themselves and women sport beards as a form of cyber-resistance to the confines prescribed by the state, psycho-nationalism in Iran has been battled out as a typically bio-political dialectic between power and resistance and this battle has been inscribed onto the body and the mind. The female body in particular holds this tension and releases it as a constructive response to forms of patriarchal domination.

Hence, the story of Iranian women is a tale of intense empowerment, exactly because of the failure of psycho-nationalism to turn them into objects of bio-political power as a means to subdue (or subjectify) them. Indeed, the folkloric aspects of Iran's popular culture have a distinctively 'feminine' touch, even in the lyrics performed by men. In the popular music of LA-based singer Dariush Eghbali, for instance, Iran becomes a loving muse, a beautiful source of inspiration for betterment and resistance to injustice. In his iconic song *vatan* (homeland), Eghbali describes Iran almost in the style of a love story, a place that he and other exiled Iranians have to re-conquer even if that involves going through the pain of emotional and physical torture: *Vatan taraneye zendani* – the homeland as a prison song; *emrooze ma emrooze faryad*, today we cry out, tomorrow holds a great day of a rebirth (*fardaye ma rooze bozorge milad*). Similar emotions are expressed by popular singers inside Iran. For instance, Ali-Reza Assar speaks of *vatan* as the mother of history-making (*vatan, ey madar-e tarikhsaz*) and his everlasting love for *his*

---

[8] There has been movement in that direction. See for instance Afsaneh Najmabadi's *Women with Mustaches and Men without Beards: Gender and Sexual Anxieties in Modern Iran*, Los Angeles: University of California Press, 2005.

Iran (*eshghe javidan-e man Iran-e man*). When I had a chance to ask Dariush Eghbali what he feels about Iran at a concert in Hamburg, he replied quickly, almost intuitively: *hesse ashegi* (the feeling of love).[9] This response was not related to a hegemonic, aggressive and violent form of psycho-nationalism. It seemed empathetic and caring, as if he was speaking about a lost love that he cared about without trying to possess her. Interestingly, when Ayatollah Khomeini was asked how he felt upon returning to Iran he famously answered 'nothing'. His whole discourse about Iran was aloof, utilitarian littered with theological terms and authoritarian prescriptions. The nation as a feminised object has a long tradition in nationalist literature of course, and psycho-nationalists routinely represent the state as the chaperone, male guardian of the vulnerable, feminised nation.[10] Yet, my point is that femininity in Iran is not merely gender-based. Iranian popular culture, philosophy, art and poetry hold a positive, life-affirming sensual, empathetic and sensitive tradition that goes beyond strict delineations of sex. Hence, my emphasis on trans-sexuality. The nation in this interpretive tradition comes out as a powerful 'transvestite', rather than a weak subject. This immensely fascinating interpretation of the meaning of Iran is one of the reasons why psycho-nationalism in the country has failed. From this perspective, the Iranian nation escapes even strict gender definitions.

Subversive intellectual tremors like this are affected, if not determined by equally tectonic shifts in global thought. Successive Iranian states have failed to coin a compliant political subject in the country despite the psycho-nationalists' assaults, because Iran as an idea and lived reality is embedded in global structures that transcend the boundaries of psycho-nationalist thinking. The subject of psycho-nationalism in Iran emerges out of the profoundly emotive discourse of Persian-centric and Islamo-centric narratives in the country. It

---

[9] Hamburg, 4 October 2014.
[10] See more recently Gayatri Chakravorty Spivak, *Nationalism and the Imagination*, London: Seagull Books, 2015.

hails the hymns and myths of authenticity, much like the German romanticists who were inspired by the writings of Herder and Fichte and the Hegelian imperative of the 'superior German nation'. Events in Iran have not been unique or typical of some sort of 'Oriental/ Muslim mentality'. I have discussed at the beginning of this study how since the eighteenth century there developed in Europe a dominant discourse that represented the state as more than a functional institution to organise the relationship between the aristocracy, the church and the nation. In the writings of Fichte, Ranke, Hegel, Herder, Mill, Mazzini and others, the state is conceptualised as a normative concept, as a polity that is destined to fulfil a higher mission – 'A nation is a soul, a spiritual principle,' as Renan puts it.[11] In Europe, the nation-state emerged as a normative, almost spiritual invention filled with a Hegelian *Geist*, spirit or consciousness. According to Hegel, the 'nation state (*das Volk als Staat*) is the spirit in its substantial rationality and immediate actuality, and is therefore the absolute power on earth'.[12]

It is true that the engineering of the national narrative in Iran has been similarly dependent on mystification and romanticised notions of the 'self'. Yet the corpus of writings that have established the discursive habitat for the 'Aryan subject' in the national imagination of the country precedes and supersedes the period of European modernity which impinged, via the discourse of Orientalism, on the way Iran has been defined. To be more precise, when during the Pahlavi dynasty Iranian scholars and the state itself adopted a scientific discourse that was meant to 'prove' the purity of the Aryan race, they were not only reacting to the Orientalist theses expressed, among others, by Count de Gobineau and Ernest Renan, who argued that Persians are racially superior to the Arabs and other 'Semitic races' because of their 'Indo-European' heritage. True, forerunners of

---

[11] Ernest Renan, 'What Is a Nation', text of a conference delivered at the Sorbonne on 11 March 1882. Available at http://ucparis.fr/files/9313/6549/9943/What_is_a_Nation.pdf (accessed 12 June 2016).
[12] Ibid.

the Aryan myth in Iran, cultural luminaries such as the aforementioned Akhundzadeh and Kermani, did internalise Orientalist notions of racial purity and introduced these ideas to the intellectual life of late nineteenth century Persia. But there was also 'Occidentalist' breeding ground for such narratives to gain currency among the intelligentsia of the country, a whole range of nationalist myths which have survived throughout the centuries and which have been repeatedly tapped into in order to define, somewhat metaphysically, the national narrative in Iran.

Equally, the re-engineering of the meaning of Islam after the revolution of 1979 cannot be divorced from the interaction between Islam and the 'west', not least via the violence of colonialism/imperialism especially between the eighteenth and twentieth century. However, this dialectic has created a particular form of disjunctive synthesis in which the Muslim 'self' and the western 'other' are entirely conjoined. It is true that the 'Muslim subject' that emerges out of the turmoil of the revolution and the subsequent devastating war between Iran and Iraq (1980–8) does not speak to the western side in order to mitigate conflict, but to accentuate difference. Revolutionary Iran has been adamant about defining the Islamic Republic in strict juxtaposition to the 'west' in general and the United States in particular. This discourse has suggested a bifurcated syntactical order within which the fundamental boundary between subject and object, self and other, has been cemented with layers and layers of narrated inventions, all of which were meant to solidify the fundamental difference between Iran and the west. Yet this political independence of Iran has been achieved via a discursive dependency. By defining Iran's new 'self' in relation to the American 'other', the discourse of the Islamic Republic has become entirely dependent on invented images of the United States in particular and the concept of the 'west' more generally. Thus an oppressive syntactical dependency has been created which demands that Iran takes the United States and the west permanently into account at each and every twist and turn of the country's official political discourse: *Marg bar Amrika* (death to America), *marg bar engelis* (death to England), *marg bar Israel* (death to Israel); calling for the 'death' of America, Israel and Britain guarantees their syntactical existence in the here and now. So the 'west' has a rather pronounced presence in Islamic Iran indeed, particularly among the right wing, the mainstay supporters of psycho-nationalism who utter those slogans with particular vehemence and ideological conviction.[13]

CRITIQUE AND MY OBJECT(IVE)

There is something very alluring about studying a country such as Iran. Of course, there are aesthetics and high culture in abundance, a national narrative that is imagined and invented with a lot of civilisational stamina. The siren song of Persia chimes with the poetry of Khayyam, Hafiz, Rabia Balkhi and Rumi and the imagination of imperial grandeur that has animated Iranian nationalists since the ancient empire of Cyrus. Persia staged as an opera would have a strong cast of heroes and villains. Many Iranians would nominate Rostam as the ultimate champion. He is the central character from the book of kings which I have discussed extensively in this book. Others would opt for Imam Hossein, the grandson of the prophet Mohammad whose killing at the battle of Kerbala in 680 AD sustains Iran's Shia imagery. This idea of Iran was embedded into the national narrative by the Safavids in the sixteenth century, as we have established in the first couple of chapters. The cast for the villains would be equally competitive: the forces of evil embodied by the Zoroastrian 'spirit of destruction', Ahriman or the 'forces of arrogance' (*mostakbaran*) represented by Yazid in the aforementioned killing of Hossein in the seventh century. For many Iranians the stage for this opera would have to be adorned with props that resemble the architectural splendour of Isfahan, Persepolis and Shiraz. Iran, for sure, is a highly

---

[13] See further Arshin Adib-Moghaddam, 'Discourse and Violence: The Friend–Enemy Conjunction in Contemporary Iranian–American Relations', *Critical Studies on Terrorism*, Vol. 2, No. 3, 2009, pp. 512–26.

prized and competitive object, not least because as an idea, the country has been imagined since antiquity.

I have tried to show in this book that it is exactly that: imagination. Nations are not primordial; they do not simply exist beyond inventions of the mind and the pen. An opera about Iran is exactly that – it *stages* an idea about Iran, in the same way as governments and their interlocutors do. For instance, from the perspective of European Orientalists, Iran was routinely represented as an exotic place, a prized colonial trophy, the epitome of Scheherazade's dream of 1,001 nights or simply a convenient supplier of oil. There was a reason why Orientalists did not bother with questions of philosophy, theory and method. Either, Iran had to be narrated to imperialists, oil companies and colonial functionaries or it was an indulgence, an exciting theme park to be desired. There was no room for philosophy or critical analysis in this constellation. What we may call 'traditional' Iranian studies suffered from comparable theoretical amnesia. Iran was narrowed down to philological platitudes, cultural simplifications or geopolitical descriptions: Persian as an Indo-European language, Iranians as semi-Aryan racial brethren and Iran as a nodal point for western imperialism.

But what Iran 'is', is entirely dependent on who speaks for it. For many Iranians today, Iran is all about Shia Islam. For many others, the true Iranian spirit can only be found in the archives of the country's pre-Islamic history. Traditional Iranian studies do not address the question of authorship, which is central to such battles over 'identity'. Rather, it contributes to contracting the meaning of Iran. There are dozens of histories of Iran out there, but only a handful address how and by whom those histories were written in the first place. History is always also *for* someone. The passion play of Hossein serves a Shia identity that entered Iran (then a majority Sunni country) through the Turkic, Safavid dynasty as indicated. Ferdowsi was dependent on the whims of Iran's Ghaznavid rulers, and the patrimony of the court and its underbelly. The point is that identities are invented in accordance with context and that they change their meaning almost immediately after their invention. Traditional Iranian studies do not challenge such questions. Yet demystifying 'origins' is important to understanding and explaining a country whose historical imagination claims several millennia of global history. Without such 'deconstruction', we end up in an unscholarly battle over identity, which confuses the audience: the opera of Rostam is staged in one room and the passion play of Hossein in the other. Here, 'critical Iranian studies' interrogate the directors and producers of both plays in order to find out how the two stages could be merged into one. This would be as giant a production as the ancient idea of the meaning of Iran merits. And ultimately, this colossal performance would be closer to appreciating the complex historiography of the country: Iran as an open parenthesis; Iran as a global idea and Iran in the middle of the crossroads of identities, a central focal point in a common human experience.

What I have so comfortably called 'critical Iranian studies' appreciate Iran as a global idea that cannot be confined to confessional or nationalistic narratives. As I have tried to demonstrate: There are traces of Iran everywhere in the world and the meaning of the country has been written beyond geography, territory and borderlines. Iran is global. There has been movement in the field of Iranian studies to appreciate that globality of the meaning of Iran. For instance, the increasingly influential MA in Iranian Studies at SOAS embraces a multidisciplinary approach that is characteristic of the SOAS brand in the social sciences. Moreover, new and influential book series published by Cambridge University Press and Bloomsbury emphasise the merits of this new approach, not only for Iranian Studies but for Middle Eastern Studies as well.[14] In Iran itself, students are experimenting with new theories and disciplines such as global thought, comparative philosophies and global history. I have been mentoring dozens of Iranian students at the best

---

[14] See Lucian Stone and Jason Bahbak Mohaghegh's book series for Bloomsbury entitled 'Suspensions: Contemporary Middle Eastern and Islamicate Thought'. Professor Ali Mirsepassi (New York University) and I have edited the book series 'The Global Middle East' for Cambridge University Press.

departments in the country and it is my impression that that there exists a new movement that is dissatisfied with the tired 'nationalism versus religion' dichotomy of the older generation. From those perspectives, Iran embraces a place beyond destinations and origins.

The thirteenth century mystic Jalaledin Rumi understood the perils of self-confining identities. In many ways, he was the Michel Foucault of his age: 'What can I do, Muslims?' he asked audaciously. 'I do not know myself. I am neither Christian nor Jew, neither Magian nor Muslim, I am not from east or west. My place is placeless, my trace is traceless.' Rumi returned from where the guardians of identity are heading. He exorcised the myth of origins and primordial existence from his mind. For many nations (and individuals) this is a perilous task. It is literally unsettling. But once we pull the self (national or individual) together and start the process of picking up the pieces, they will appear clearer to us; we will be able to analyse and comprehend ourselves more easily and to reconfigure our relationships within a rather more tolerant frame than before. The poetry of Rumi is universally loved exactly because it transcends, it is not bound by hysterical calls for identity. Psycho-nationalism, on the other hand, reduces and discriminates; it is partisan and intimidating. If world peace continues to be the aim of humanity, the horizon of a new kind of thinking and a new type of society must be this open mind of the poet and critical philosopher.

Politics simulates reality, but it is never simultaneous with reality. If politics is the art of invention and deception then it is the task of philosophy and critical practice to reveal and dislocate the elements of construction, outright lies or mythologies, not least as a civil responsibility to ensure democratic and pluralistic supervision of the state. Such are the ingredients of a permanent counter-culture furthering love, peace and empathy. This book was informed and intended to bolster those principles and anyone can further them through their own means and in their own lives on a daily basis. My approach in global thought and comparative philosophies has demonstrated the entanglement of Iran with global history and the inevitable trans-geographic dynamics that the idea of Iran provokes and entails. These were my humble tools and they were chosen in order to carve out a wider canvas for the meaning of Iran and, by extension, of any national narrative. Tolerant scholarship creates acceptance through inclusion. It provides an alternative to the killing mentality characteristic of psycho-nationalist thinking. Individuals are rarely, if ever mad, but national hysteria stoked up by politicians has repeatedly transmuted into insanity. In an era that is veering towards new forms of fascism, we need more freedoms to think. I hope this book will be considered an incitement to that end.

Bibliography

Abisaab, Rula Jurdi, *Converting Persia: Religion and Power in the Safavid Empire*, London: I.B. Tauris, 2004.

Abrahamian, Ervand, *A History of Modern Iran*, Cambridge: Cambridge University Press, 2008.

The Coup 1953, the CIA and the Roots of Modern US-Iranian Relations, New York: New Press, 2013.

Adib-Moghaddam, Arshin, 'Global Intifadah? September 11th and the Struggle within Islam', *Cambridge Review of International Affairs*, Vol. 15, No. 2 (2002), pp. 203–16.

'Islamic Utopian Romanticism and the Foreign Policy Culture of Iran', *Middle East Critique*, Vol. 14, No. 3 (2005), pp. 265–92.

'A (Short) History of the Clash of Civilisations', *Cambridge Review of International Affairs*, Vol. 21, No. 2 (2006), pp. 217–34.

'The Pluralistic Momentum in Iran and the Future of the Reform Movement', *Third World Quarterly*, Vol. 27, No. 4 (2006), pp. 665–74.

'Discourse and Violence: The Friend-Enemy Conjunction in Contemporary Iranian-American Relations', *Critical Studies on Terrorism*, Vol. 2, No. 3 (2009), pp. 512–26.

'What Is Radicalism? Power and Resistance in Iran', *Middle East Critique*, Vol. 21, No. 3 (2012), pp. 271–90.

On the Arab Revolts and the Iranian Revolution: Power and Resistance Today, New York: Bloomsbury, 2013.

(ed.), *A Critical Introduction to Khomeini*, Cambridge: Cambridge University Press, 2014.

'Global Grandeur and the Idea of Iran', in Henner Fuertig (ed.), *Regional Power in the Middle East*, London: Palgrave, 2014, pp. 43–58.

'Remnants of Empire: Civilisation, Torture and Racism in the War on Rerrorism', in Michael Patrick Cullinane and David Ryan (eds.), *US Foreign Policy and the Other*, New York: Berghahn, 2014, pp. 222–34.

Adorno, Theodor W., *The Culture Industry: Selected Essays on Mass Culture*, London: Routledge, 1991.

Agamben, Giorgio, *State of Exception*, Chicago: University of Chicago Press, 2005.

Ahmadi, Hamid, 'Islam and Nationalism in Contemporary Iranian Society and Politics,' *Iranian Review of Foreign Affairs*, Vol. 1, No. 1 (2010), pp. 193–221.

Al-e Ahmad, Jalal, *Plagued by the West (Gharbzadegi)*, trans. Paul Sprachman, New York: Caravan, 1982.

Alexander, Jeffrey C., *Performance and Power*, London: Polity Press, 2011.

Algar, Hamid, 'A Short Biography', in Abdar Rahman Koya (ed.), *Imam Khomeini: Life, Thought and Legacy*, Petaling Jaya: Islamic Book, 2009.

Ali, Latife Reda, *Khomeini's Discourse of Resistance: The Discourse of Power of the Islamic Revolution*, PhD thesis, London: School of Oriental and African Studies, 2012.

Amir-Moezzi, Ali, *The Divine Guide in Early Shi'ism: The Sources of Esotericism in Islam*, trans. David Streight, Albany: State University of New York Press, 1994.

Anderson, Benedict, *Imagined Communities: Reflections on the Origin and Spread of Nationalism*, London: Verso, 2016.

Ansari, Ali, *The Politics of Nationalism in Modern Iran*, Cambridge: Cambridge University Press, 2012.

Antliff, Mark, *Avant-Garde Fascism: The Mobilisation of Myth, Art and Culture in France, 1909–1939*, Durham: Duke University Press, 2007.

Ardlc, Nurullah, 'Genealogy or Asabiyya? Ibn Khaldun between Arab Nationalism and the Ottoman Caliphate', *Journal of Near Eastern Studies*, Vol. 71, No. 2 (2 October 2012), pp. 315–24.

Arjomand, Said Amir, *The Turban for the Crown: The Islamic Revolution in Iran*, Oxford: Oxford University Press, 1989.

Asgharzadeh, Alireza, *Iran and the Challenge of Diversity: Islamic Fundamentalism, Aryanist, Racism and Democratic Struggles*, New York: Palgrave Macmillan, 2007.

Azimi, Fakhreddin, *The Quest for Democracy in Iran: A Century of Struggle against Authoritarian Rule*, Cambridge, MA: Harvard University Press, 2010.

Bazargan, Mehdi, 'Religion and Liberty', in Charles Kurzman (ed.), *Liberal Islam: A Sourcebook*, Oxford: Oxford University Press, 1998, pp. 73–84.

Bergman, Ernst, *Fichte und der Nationalsozialismus*, Breslau: Walter Gehl und Johann Koch, 1933.

Bhabha, Homi K., *The Location of Culture*, London: Routledge, 1994.

Bilgin, Pinar, 'Whose "Middle East"? Geopolitical Inventions and Practices of Security', *International Relations*, Vol. 18, No. 1 (2004), pp. 25–41.

Boroujerdi, Mehrzad, *Iranian Intellectuals and the West: The Tormented Triumph of Nativism*, Syracuse: Syracuse University Press, 1996.

Buchta, Wilfried, 'The Failed Pan-Islamic Program of the Islamic Republic: Views of the Liberal Reformers of the Religious "Semi-Opposition"', in Nikki R.

Keddie and Rudi Matthee (eds.), *Iran and the Surrounding World: Interactions in Culture and Cultural Politics*, Seattle: University of Washington Press, 2002.

Chittick, William C., *The Sufi Path of Knowelge: Ibn Al-Arabi's Metaphysics of Imagination*, Albany: State University of New York Press, 1989.

Cleveland, William L., *The Making of an Arab Nationalist: Ottomanism and Arabism in the Life and Thought of Sati' al-Husri*, Princeton: Princeton University Press, 1971.

Cole, Juan R. I., 'Iranian Culture and South Asia, 1500–1900', in Nikki R. Keddie and Rudi Matthee (eds.), *Iran and the Surrounding World: Interactions in Culture and Cultural Politics*, Seattle: University of Washington Press, 2002, pp. 15–35.

Dabashi, Hamid, *Post-Orientalism: Knowledge and Power in a Time of Terror*, London: Transaction Publishers, 2009.

Shi'ism: A Religion of Protest, Cambridge: Harvard University Press, 2011.

The World of Persian Literary Humanism, Cambridge: Harvard University Press, 2012.

Davari, Mahmood T., *The Political Thought of Ayatollah Murtaza Mutahhari: An Iranian Theoretician of the Islamic State*, London: Routledge, 2005.

Davies, Dick, 'Iran and Aniran: The Shaping of a Legend', in Abbas Amanat and Farzin Vejdani (eds.), *Iran Facing Others: Identity Boundaries in a Historical Perspective*, London: Palgrave, 2012, pp. 39–50.

Ebtekar, Massoumeh, *Takeover in Tehran: The Inside Story of the 1979 U.S. Embassy Capture*, Vancouver: Talon, 2000.

Elling, Rasmus Christian, *Minorities in Iran: Nationalism and Ethnicity after Khomeini*, New York: Palgrave Macmillan, 2013.

Falasca-zamponi, Simonetta, *Fascist Spectacle: The Aesthetics of Power in Mussolini's Italy*, London: University of California Press, 2000.

Fallaci, Oriana, *Interview with History*, New York: Houghton-Mifflin, 1977.

Foucault, Michel, *The Birth of Biopolitics: Lectures at the College de France, 1978–1979*, New York: Palgrave Macmillan, 2010.

Freud, Sigmund, *The Complete Psychological Works of Sigmund Freud*, Vol. 18, London: Vintage, 2001.

Fullam, Simon Levis, *Giuseppe Mazzini and the Origins of Fascism*, New York: Palgrave Macmillan, 2015.

Ghamari-Tabrizi, Behrooz, *Foucault in Iran: Islamic Revolution after the Enlightenment*, Minneapolis: University of Minnesota Press, 2016.

Goody, Jack, *Renaissances: The One or the Many?* Cambridge: Cambridge University Press, 2010.

Hazin, Muhammed Ali, *The Life of Sheikh Mohammed Ali Hazin*, trans. Francis C. Belfour, London: Oriental Translation Fund, 1830.

Hobsbawm, Eric, *Nations and Nationalism since 1780*, Cambridge: Cambridge University Press, 2nd edition, 2012.

Hobsbawm, Eric and Terence Ranger (eds.), *The Invention of Tradition*, Cambridge: Cambridge University Press, 2012.

Hutchinson, John and Anthony D. Smith (eds.), *Nationalism*, Oxford: Oxford University Press, 1994.

Jahanbegloo, Ramin, *The Gandhian Moment*, Cambridge: Harvard University Press, 2013.

Jamshidi, Mohammad-Hossein (ed.), *Andishey-e Siasiy-e Imam Khomeini*, Tehran: Pajoheshkade-ye imam Khomeini va enghelabe islami, 1384 [2005].

Kadivar, Mohsen, 'Freedom of Religion and Belief in Islam', in Mehran Kamrava (ed.), *The New Voices of Islam: Reforming Politics and Modernity*, London: I.B. Tauris, 2006.

al-Karaki, Muhaqiq, *Jameal Maqasid*, Vol. 2, Qum: AhlolBayt Publication, 1365 [1986].

Kashani-Sabet, Firoozeh, *Frontier Fictions: Shaping the Iranian Nation 1804–1946*, Princeton: Princeton University Press, 1999.

Keddie, Nikki R., *Religion and Politics in Iran: Shi'ism from Quietism to Revolution*, New Haven: Yale University Press, 1983.

Khaldun, Ibn, *The Muqaddimah: An Introduction to History*, Vol. 1, trans. Franz Rosenthal, Princeton: Princeton University Press, 1989.

Khamene'i, Ali, *Manifestation of the Islamic Spirit*, trans. Mahliqa Qara'i and Laleh Bakhtiar, Markham: Open Press, 1991.

Khamene'i, Sayyid Ali, *Iqbal: The Poet Philosopher of Islamic Resurgence*. Speech delivered at the opening session of the First International Conference on Iqbal, held at Tehran, 10–12 March 1986, on the occasion of the 108th birth anniversary of the poet of the Subcontinent. Trans. Mahliqa Qara'i. Available at <http://islam-pure.de/imam/books/iqbal.htm> Accessed 12 November 2013.

Khomeini, Rouhollah, *Islam and Revolution: Writings and Declarations of Imam Khomeini (1941–1980)*, Hamid Algar (ed. & trans.), Berkeley: Mizan Press, 1981.

Khomeini, Ruhollah, *Shou'n va Ekhtiyarate Valiye Faqih*, Tehran: Vezarat-e Ershade Islami, 1986.

Ain-e enghelab-e Islami: Gozidehai az andisheh va ara-ye Imam Khomeini, Tehran: Moasses-ye tanzim va naschr-e assar-e Imam Khomeini, 1373 [1994].

Al Makaseb al Muharrama, vol. ii, Tehran: The Institute for Compilation and Publication of Imam Khomeini's Work, 1995.

Khomeini, Ruhiollah, *Sahifeh-ye Iman (Sahifeh-ye Nur, vol. x): An Athology of Imam Khomeinis Speeches, Messages, Interviews, Decrees, Religious Permissions, and Letters*, Tehran: The Institute for Compilation of Imam Khomeini's Works, 2008.

Khomeini, Ruhollah, *Kashf-e Asrar*, Qom: Azadi Publications, 1943.

Kia, Mana, 'Accounting for Difference: A Comparative Look at the Autobiographical Travel Narratives of Hazin Lahiji and Abd-al-Karim Kashmiri', *Journal of Persianate Studies*, Vol. 2 (2009), pp. 210–36.

Knysh, Alexander, 'Irfan Revisited: Khomeini and the Legacy of Islamic Mystical Philosophy', *The Middle East Journal*, Vol. 64, No. 4 (1992), pp. 631–53.

Mahdi, Muhsin S., *AlFarabi and the Foundation of Islamic Political Philosophy*, Chicago: University of Chicago Press, 2010.

Malesevic, Sinisa, 'Where Does Group Solidarity Come From? Gellner and Ibn Khaldun Revisited', *Thesis Eleven: Critical Theory and Historical Sociology*, Vol. 129, No. 1, 2015, pp. 85–99.

Marx, Anthony W., *Faith in Nation: Exclusionary Origins of Nationalism*, Oxford: Oxford University Press, 2005.

Marashi, Afshin, *Nationalising Iran: Culture, Power, and the State, 1870–1940*, Seattle: University of Washington Press, 2008.

'The Nation's Poet: Ferdowsi and the Iranian National Imagination', in Touraj Atabaki (ed.), *Iran in the 20th Century: Historiography and Political Culture*, London: I.B. Tauris, 2009, pp. 93–111.

Massad, Joseph, *Islam in Liberalism*, Chicago: University of Chicago Press, 2015.

Matthee, Rudi, *Persia in Crisis: Safavid Decline and the Fall of Isfahan*, London: I.B. Tauris, 2011.

Mayall, James, *Nationalism and International Society*, Cambridge: Cambridge University Press, 1990.

Mazzini, Guiseppe, 'To the Young Men of Italy', in Lewis Copeland, Lawrence W. Lamm and Stephen J. McKenna (eds.), *The World's Great Speeches*, Mineola: Dover Publications, 1999, pp. 98–102.

Meisami, Julie Scott, *Structure and Meaning in Medieval Arabic and Persian Lyric Poetry: Orient Pearls*, London: Routledge, 2002.

Mir-Hosseini, Ziba, *Islam and Gender: The Religious Debate in Contemporary Iran*, London: I.B. Tauris, 2000.

Mirsepassi, Ali, *Political Islam, Iran and the Enlightenment: Philosophies of Hope and Despair*, Cambridge: Cambridge University Press, 2010.

Transnationalism in Iranian Political Thought: The Life and Times of Ahmad Fardid (The Global Middle East), Cambridge: Cambridge University Press, 2017.

Moazzen, Matyam, 'Rituals of Commemoration, Rituals of Self-Invention: Safavid Religious Colleges, and the Collective Memory of the Shia', *Iranian Studies*, Vol. 49, No. 4 (2016), pp. 555–75.

Mohaghegh, Jason Bahbak, *Silence in Middle Eastern and Western Thought: The Radical Unspoken*, London: Routledge, 2013.

Moin, Baqer, *Khomeini: Life of the Ayatollah*, London: I.B. Tauris, 1999.

Mudiam, Prithvi Ram, *India and the Middle East*, London: I.B. Tauris, 1994.

Najmabadi, Afsaneh, *Women with Mustaches and Men without Beards: Gender and Sexual Anxieties in Modern Iran*, Los Angeles: University of California Press, 2005.

Netton, Ian Richard (ed.), *Orientalism Revisited: Art, Land and Voyage*, London: Routledge, 2013.

Newman, Andrew J., *Safavid Iran: Rebirth of a Persian Empire*, London: I.B. Tauris, 2006.

Pahlavi, Mohammad Reza, *Mission for My Country*, New York: McGraw-Hill, 1961.

Pande, Aparna, *Explaining Pakistan's Foreign Policy: Escaping India*, London: Routledge, 2011.

Pistor-Hatam, Anja, 'Writing Back? Jalal Al-e Ahmad's (1923–69) Reflections on Selected Periods of Iranian History', *Iranian Studies*, Vol. 40, No. 5 (December 2007), pp. 559–78.

Rahimi, Babak and David M. Faris, *Social Media in Iran: Politics and Society after 2009*, Albany: State University of New York Press, 2015.

Rahnema, Ali, *An Islamic Utopian: A Political Biography of Ali Shariati*, London: I.B. Tauris, 2000.

Rash, Felicity, *German Images of the Self and the Other: Nationalist, Colonialist and Anti-semitic Discourse 1871–1918*, New York: Palgrave Macmillan, 2012.

Rezun, Miron M. *The Iranian Crisis of 1941: The Actors, Britain, Germany, and the Soviet Union*, Wien: Böhlau, 1982.

Rizvi, Kishwar, *The Safavid Dynastic Shrine: Architecture, Religion and Power in Early Modern Iran*, London: I.B. Tauris, 2011.

Robinson, Francis, *Islam in South Asia: Oxford Bibliographies Online Research Guide*, Oxford: Oxford University Press, 2010.

Roy, Olivier, *The Failure of Political Islam*, trans. Carole Volk, Cambridge: Harvard University Press, 1996.

Ryad, Umar, 'Anti-imperialism and the Pan-Islamic Movement', in David Motadel (ed.), *Islam and the European Empires*, Oxford: Oxford University Press, 2014, pp. 131–49.

Sachedina, Abdulaziz Abdulhussein, *The Just Ruler in Shi'ite Islam: The Comprehensive Authority of the Jurist in Imamite Jurisprudence*, Oxford: Oxford University Press, 1998.

Safamanesh, Kamran, 'Architectural Historiography, 1921–1942', in Touraj Atabaki (ed.), *Iran in the 20th Century: Historiography and Political Culture*, London: I.B. Tauris, 2009, pp. 121–53.

Said, Edward, *Orientalism*, London: Penguin, 1995.

Covering Islam: How the Media and the Experts Determine How We See the Rest of the World, London: Vintage, 1997.

Saleh, Alam, *Ethnic Identity and the State in Iran*, New York: Palgrave Macmillan, 2013.

Savory, Roger M., 'Safavids', in Peter Burke, Irfan Habib and Halil İnalcık (eds.), *History of Humanity-Scientific and Cultural Development: From the Sixteenth to the Eighteenth Century*, London: Taylor & Francis, 1999.

Schirazi, Asghar, *The Constitution of Iran: Politics and the State in the Islamic Republic*, trans. John O' Kane, London: I.B. Tauris, 1998.

Sevea, Iqbal Singh, *The Political Philosophy of Muhammad Iqbal: Islam and Nationalism in Late Colonial India*, Cambridge: Cambridge University Press, 2012.

Shayegan, Dariush, *Cultural Schizophrenia: Islamic Societies Confronting the West*, Syracuse: Syracuse University Press, 1997.

Sherratt, Yvonne, *Hitler's Philosophers*, New Haven: Yale University Press, 2013.

Sikand, Yoginder S., 'The Jama'at-i-Islami of Jammu and Kashmir', in Paul R. Brass and Achin Vanaik (eds.), *Competing Nationalisms in South Asia: Essays for Asghar Ali Engineer*, London: Sangam Books Ltd., 2002.

Sina, Ibn, 'Fontes sapientiae (uyun al-hikmah)', in Abdurrahman Badawied (ed.), *uyun al-hikmah*, Cairo: no publisher, 1954.

Soroush, Abdolkarim, *Reason, Freedom and Democracy in Islam: Essential Writings of Abdolkarim Soroush*, in Mahmoud Sadri and Ahmad Sadri (eds. & trans.), Oxford: Oxford University Press, 2000.

Spivak, Gayatri Chakravorty, *Nationalism and the Imagination*, London: Seagull Books, 2015.

Stone, Lucian (ed.), *Iranian Identity and Cosmopolitanism: Spheres of Belonging*, New York: Bloomsbury, 2014.

Tabatabai, Sadegh, *Khaterat-e siasi – ejtemai-ye doktor Sadegh Tabatabai, jelde aval*, vol. i, Tehran: Mo'aseseh-ye chap va nashr-e oruj, 1387 [2008].

Taleqani, Ayatollah Mahmud, 'The Characteristics of Islamic Economics', in John J. Donohue and John L. Esposito (eds.), *Islam in Transition: Muslim Perspectives*, Oxford: Oxford University Press, 2007.

Tavakoli-Targhi, Mohamad, 'Early Persianate Modernity', in Sheldon Pollock (ed.), *Forms of Knowledge in Early Modern Asia: Explorations in the Intellectual History of India and Tibet, 1500–1800*, Durham: Duke University Press, 2011.

Tazmini, Ghoncheh, *Khatami's Iran: The Islamic Republic and the Turbulent Path to Reform*, London: I.B Tauris, 2009.
——— *Revolution and Reform in Russia and Iran: Modernisation and Politics in Revolutionary States*, London: I.B. Tauris, 2012.
——— 'The Persian-Portuguese Encounter in Hormuz: Orientalism Reconsidered', *Iranian Studies*, Vol. 50, No. 2 (2017), pp. 271–92.
Tibi, Bassam, *Arab Nationalism: Between Islam and the Nation-State*, New York: Palgrave Macmillan, 1997.
Walbridge, Linda, *The Most Learned of the Shi'a: The Institution of the Marja' Taqlid*, Oxford: Oxford University Press, 2001.
Walzer, Richard, *Greek into Arabic: Essays on Islamic Philosophy*, Cambridge: Harvard University Press, 1962.
Yaghmaian, Behzad, *Social Change in Iran: An Eyewitness Account of Dissent, Defiance, and New Movements for Rights*, New York: State University of New York Press, 2002.
Yarshater, Ehsan, 'Persian Identity in Historical Perspective', *Iranian Studies*, Vol. 26, No. 1–2 (2007), pp. 141–2.
Zastoupil, Lynn and Martin Moir (eds.), *The Great Indian Education Debate: Documents Relating to the Orientalist-Anglicist Controversy, 1781–1843*, London: Routledge, 2013.
Zia-Ebrahimi, Reza, *The Emergence of Iranian Nationalism: Race and the Politics of Dislocation*, New York: Columbia University Press, 2016.
(Ziarati), Seyyed Hamid Rouhani, *Baresi va tahlil az nehzate Imam Khomeini*, 11th edition, Tehran: Entesharat-e Rahe Imam, 1360 [1982].

Index

Abduh, Muhammad, 112, 129
Achaemenid style, 43
adibs, 42–3
Adorno, Theodor, 16
Afghani, Jamal-ad din, 112
al-Afghani, Jamaladin, 128–9
Afghanistan, 85
Aflaq, Michel, 29
Agamben, Giorgio, 2
Ahmadinejad, Mahmoud, 16, 35, 119–20
Akbar, 70
al-e Ahmad, Jalal, 56–7, 58–9, 61
Anderson, Benedict, 5, 6, 9
Anglo Iranian Oil Company, 78, 129–30
anti-colonialism, 80
anti-imperialism, 82
antiquarian Sassanid style, 43
Arab nationalism, 29
architectural styles, 43–5, 54–5, 70
Aristotle, 27
Aryanism, 51–6, 76, 112
Asadabadi, 128–9
Ataturk, 5

Bahar, Muhammad Taqi, 76
al-Banna, Hassan, 105
Bazargan, Mehdi, 97, 131–2, 132, 134–5, 140, 141
bazgasht be khish (return to the self), 58–60
Begum, Halima, 38
Bergman, Ernst, 23
Berhman, Ernst, 22
Bidel, 70, 73
bio-power, 10–11
Biruni, Abu Raihan, 70
Bismarck, Otto von, 23
Bonyad-e Mostafazan, 48
Boroujerdi, Hussein, 102
Britannia, 1
Browne, Edward B., 76

Camoes, Luis, Vaz de, 36–7
CENTO (Central Treaty Organisation), 76–7, 81
colonialism, 71
constitution of Islamic Republic of Iran, 92, 115–16
Constitutional Revolt, 106
cosmopolitanism, 22
Cultural Revolution Council, 135
Cultural Revolution Institute, 135
Cyrus cylinder, 10, 35
Cyrus II, 10

Dabashi, Hamid, 33, 73, 148
Darius the Great, 33
Dastgheib, Ayatollah, 119
Davies, Dick, 32
al-Dawlah, Mumtahin, 75

eastern spirituality, 80
Ebtekar, Masoumeh, 63
Eghbali, Dariush, 4, 149
English Education Act of 1835, 74
Eshkevari, Hojatoleslam Hassan Yusef, 66, 135, 140
export of the revolution, 50

Farabi, 104, 105, 106
Fardid, Ahmad, 58
farvahar, 34
Fatima is Fatima (Shariati), 63
feminism, 148–9
Ferdowsi, 30–2, 34, 36, 37, 39, 72
Fichte, Johann Gottlieb von, 21–3, 25
foreign policy
    and identity, 46–7
    pro-American, 76–7
foreign policy culture, 47–51
Foucault, Michel, 10–11, 156
free will, 11
freedom
    and Islam, 127, 130–5
    meaning of in Iran, 125–6

Freedom Movement of Iran, 131, 133
Freud, Sigmund, 14

Gabrielli di Quercita, Nicolo, 46
Gandhi, Indira, 81, 82
Garibaldi, Giuseppe, 20
Garshapnameh (The epic of Gershap), 72
Gellner, Ernest, 28
German language, 22
Germany, 16, 21-3
Gewaltmonopol, 2
Gandhi, 77-8
gharbzadegi (or westtoxification), 58-9, 60
Gobineau, 76
Googoosh, 7
Gorbachov, Mikhail, 105
Green Movement, 16
Guardian Council, 116

Haeri, Abdolkarim, 99
Haeri, Ayatollah, 102
Hazin, Mohammad Ali, 71-3
historical memory, 75
Hitler, Adolf, 53
Hobsbawm, Eric, 3-4, 5, 6, 15
Höldeke, Theodor, 31
Hossein, Imam, 153
Hossein, Mir-Hamed, 99
hosseiniyeh, 35
Hoveyda, Amir Abbas, 97
Human Rights Association of Iran, 131
humanism, 148
Al-Husri, Sati, 29-30
Hussein, Saddam, 82

Ibn Arabi, 104, 105, 106
Ibn Khaldun, 26-9, 31
Ibn Sina, 104, 105, 106, 142, 143-4
identity
    and foreign policy, 46-7
    and psycho-nationalism, 23-4, 33-4
    and *shahnameh*, 31-2
    psycho-nationalism as source of, 14
identity construction, 80
identity politics of Islamic revolution of 1979, 65-8
Imperial Tobacco Company, 128
imperialism, 126-30
India-Iran interaction
    conclusion, 87-9
    history, 69-76
    introduction to, 68-9
    rediscovery, 76-87
Indo-Iranian dialectic, 69
international relations, 45-7
    and Aryanism, 51-6
    and Islam, 56-63
    foreign policy culture of Iran, 47-51
    Iranian power, 63-8
Iqbal, Muhammad, 78-80
Iranian power in international relations, 63-8
Iran-Iraq War, 94
Islam, 55, 56-63
    and freedom, 127
    and identity politics, 65-8
    introduction to, 89-90
    liberation theology, 58
    velayat-e faqih, 66
Islamic revolution of 1979, 65-8, 126
Islamic secularism, 139-45
Israel, 86

Kadivar, Mohsen, 135, 138-9, 140, 142
al-Karaki, Muhaqiq, 41-2, 101-2
Kashf-e Asrar (Discovery of Secrets) (Khomeini), 102-4, 106, 108
Kashmir, 83
Kasravi, Ahmad, 53
Kaykavoos, King of Persia, 32
al-Kazim, Musa, 99
Kemal, Mustapha, 5
Khamenei, Ali, 10, 16, 48, 49
    and India, 81
    and Montazeri, 118-20
    appointment of, 116, 117
    as prefect of Khomeini's legacy, 119-21
    compared to Khomeini, 89-90, 114-15, 123-5
    lack of religious credentials, 117-18
    on Iqbal, 79-80
    pragmatism, 82, 118, 121
Khan, Karim, 46
Khatami, Mohammad, 83, 84, 86
Khomeini industry, 110-11
Khomeini, Ayatollah, 4, 11, 48, 49-50, 60-3, 66, 81
    and death, 93-5
    and Pakistan, 83
    at Qom, 100-1

INDEX 169

compared to Khamenei, 89–90, 114–15, 123–5
death of, 82, 109–10
divisiveness, 92–3
early life of, 98–100
influence of, 90
intellectual biography, 96–102
Iran after, 110–16
Kashf-e Asrar (*Discovery of Secrets*), 102–4
philosophy, 104–9
radicalism of, 90–2
socialisation of, 101–2
ulema (clerics), 97–8
vision of governance, 95–6, 107–9
Khomeini, Mostafa, 99
Kia, Mana, 72
Kim Jong-un, 8
koinonia, 27

language, 29–30, 54, 55, 70, 74–5
Le Pen, Marine, 13, 145
literature, 70–3, 76

Macaulay, Thomas Babington, 74–5
Marx, Karl, 20
mass communication, 9
Mawdudi, Muhammad Ala, 105
Mazzini, Giuseppe, 20–2, 25
Merkel, Angela, 8
Montazeri, Ayatollah, 116, 118–20
Mossadegh, Mohammad, 46, 77–8, 92, 107, 129–30
Muqaddimah (Ibn Khaldun), 26
Mussolini, Benito, 20

Nadir Shah, 73–4
narcissism, 14
national interest, interpretation of, 49
national languages, 5
National Museum of Iran, 43
national myths, 4
nationalised infrastructure, 38
nationalism in the West, 26
nationalistic narcissism, 45
nations as imaginary constructs, 12
Nehru, Jawaharlal, 77–8
Nehzat-e azadi-ye Iran (Freedom Movement of Iran), 97
New Delhi Declaration, 84–5

Non-Alignment Movement, 76, 81, 82
nuclear energy programme, 86–7
Nur Jahan, 70

Obama, Barack, 49
oil nationalisation, 129, 131
Orientalism, 74, 76
Orientalist themes, 30–1
Os Lusiadas (Camoes), 36
Ottoman Empire, 40

Pahlavi dynasty, 34, 35, 36, 38–9, 52, 75, 106
Pakistan, 77, 83
Persia, use of the term, 52
Persian language, 54, 55, 70, 74–5, 80–1
Persian language journals, 30–1
Persian purity, 35
political hubris, 46
Portuguese epic poem, 36–7
positive distinction, 14
power and knowledge, nexus between, 41
pragmatism, 118, 121–3
psycho-nationalism, 1, 6
    and identity, 23–4, 33–4
    and othering, 14–15
    as division creator, 16–17
    as intrusive, 11–12
    as invasive, 10–11
    as source of identity, 14
    belief in possibility of change, 25
    compared to terrorism, 37–8
    depth of in Iran, 35–6
    Eastern precedents, 26–36
    emotionalism, 24–5
    in Germany, 21–3
    in Iran, 11–12
    in Khomeini's speeches, 61–3
    nation as protective mother, 29–30
    overview of, 8–20
    potency of, 13–14
    psychological aspects, 17–18
    shahnameh, 31–4

Qutb, Sayyid, 105

racial affinity, myth of, 53
Radhakishnan, Sarvepalli, 141
Rafsanjani, Ali-Akbar Hashemi, 82, 134
Rahnema, Ali, 113

Ranger, Terence, 4
Rao, Narasimha, 82, 83
reformists, 135–9
Refuting the Criminal Invectives of Mysticism (Al-Karaki), 41
re-Islamization of Iran, 112–13
Renan, Ernest, 23–5, 76
revolution of 1979, 5, 16, 38, 46
Reza Khan, 52, 106, 129
Reza Shah, 34, 38, 54–6, 61, 63–5, 76–7, 102, 107, 130
role identity, 67
Rostam, 32, 153
Rouhani, Hassan, 90
Roy, Oliver, 114
Rumi, Jalaledin, 156

Sabke-Hendi (Indian style), 73
Sadr, Abolhasan Bani, 97
al-Sadr, Ayatollah Mohammad Baqir, 105
Sadra, Mulla, 105
Safavid dynasty, 38–43, 43–5, 68, 69, 101
Sahabi, Yadollah, 131
Said, Edward, 74
Salazar, Antonio, 36
Sassanid Iran, 9
self-designation, 51
Shah Abbas I, 41
Shah Ismail, 38–41
Shah Ismail II, 41
Shah mosque, 44
Shahabadi, Mirza Mohammad Ali, 104
shahnameh, 31–4, 36, 39
Shariati, Ali, 56–8, 59–60, 61, 63, 79, 131, 141, 147–8
Shayegan, Daryush, 6
Shia clerics, 41–2
Shia Islam, 40–1
Shirazi, Asghar, 111
Shirazi, Ayatollah Mirza Hossein, 128
Siyavash, 32
social solidarity, 27–8
Society for National Heritage, 53
Society for National Monuments, 34
Sohrawardi, 105
Soroush, Abdolkarim, 135–8, 140, 142
Soudabeh, 32
Soviet Union, 5, 83

state power, 27
state-sponsored media, 48
sudur-e enghelab, 50
Sunni Islam, 39
supreme jurisprudent, 42, 61, 89, 102, 104–5, 111, 113, 115–16, 132

Tabatabai, Sadegh, 100
Talbot, Major G., 128
Taleqani, Ayatollah Mahmoud, 131, 133–4, 140
Taliban, 85
Taqizadeh, 34
Taqizadeh, Hassan, 30–1
tawheed (unity of God), 104
Tehran Declaration, 84
The Investion of Tradition, 4
The siege of Shiraz (Gabrielli), 46
tobacco revolts, 128–9
totalitarianism, 16
Treaty of Westphalia, 39
Trump, Donald, 1, 13, 147
Turkish language, 5
Tusi, by Abu Mansour Ali ibn Ahmad, 72
Tusi, Nasir ad-Din, 56, 104

ulema (clerics), 97–8
United States
    and India, 86–7
    and Reza Shah, 63–5

vahdat al-vojud (unity of existence), 104
velayat-e faqih (rule of the Supreme Jurisprudent), 66, 89–90, 102, 105, 108, 113, 133
Virtuous City, 104

Weber, Max, 2
western imperialism, 74–5
White Revolution, 107
Wilders, Geert, 145
women, 148–50

Yarshater, Ehsan, 33
Yazid, 59–60, 98

Zoroastrianism, 7